WHY JESUS WAITS

Herbert E Douglass

Coldwater MI 49036
www.remnantpublications.com

Copyright © 2009 Remnant Publications
All Rights Reserved
Printed in the USA

Published by
Remnant Publications
649 East Chicago Road
Coldwater MI 49036
517-279-1304
www.remnantpublications.com

All scriptural references are from the Revised Standard Version, unless noted otherwise.

Bible texts credited to Phillips are from The New Testament in Modern English, © J. B. Phillips 1958. Used by permission of TheMacmillan Company.

Bible texts credited to NASB are from The New American Standard Bible, © The Lockman Foundation 1960, 1962, 1963, 1968, 1971,1972. Used by permission.

Cover Design by David Berthiaume
Cover photo by iStockphoto

ISBN 978-1-933291-47-5

Contents

Where Jesus Is Now 5

Importance of the Sanctuary Truth 17

The Historical Anchor 25

The Truth Satan Fears Most.. 35

The Mediator's Twofold Role 43

God's Purpose Through a Symbol 53

The Vindication of God... 65

Why Time Lingers 85

WHERE JESUS IS NOW

A NUMBER of years ago, most of the English-speaking world experienced a phenomenon that was as unexpected as water flowing uphill. After a decade (1960s) of the "God is Dead" emphasis, after years of campus revolutions and a firestorm attack on traditional values and authority of any kind—a curious thing happened, and of all places, first in New York City.

In the first year of its running, a Broadway play grossed $20 million and went on to earn many more millions. And the name of the play? JESUS CHRIST SUPERSTAR!

Overnight, it seemed, Jesus had made it "big" in the music industry, for other religious plays and movies followed. And He opened up a skyrocketing market in the book industry where many of the bestsellers were concerned about Him and His Second Coming.

In the chorus of JESUS CHRIST SUPERSTAR, a great question was asked: "Jesus Christ, who are You?"

Although the right answer was not given, the question is deeper than musical entertainment and broader than mere curiosity. For everyone on Planet Earth, there is nothing more important than who Jesus is, what He has done, where He is now, and what He is presently doing for the human race.

But, strange as it may seem, even Christians have been divided over the centuries as to whom He really is. They have overemphasized either His Godhood or manhood. Rarely has the real Jesus been given His rightful place. He has been described in such varied and sometimes odd terms that an interested observer feels like asking, "Will the real Jesus stand up?"

And so the great question remains: "Jesus Christ, who are You?" Who *is* He who became the focus of a "Jesus revolution" among youth of the Western world in the 1970s, perhaps the most unexpected and unpredicted event of modern times? Then again, who is He who could transform self-serving skeptics in occupied Palestine two thousand years ago into devoted followers who would live or die *for Him?*

The question, Jesus Christ, who are You? hovers above every person who seeks purpose in life or who tries to run from that inner voice that haunts with guilt. We can tune Him out. We can salute Him, while not seriously following Him. We can "use" Him by claiming His pardon, but not His power. However, we cannot really ignore Him. He is always there, like no other person who has ever lived.

But, who is He? Where did He come from? Paul, in writing his letter to the Hebrews, referred to Jesus' unique status as mankind's "pioneer" (chapter 12:2) and to His human record that permitted Him to be regarded as humanity's "perfect leader": "It was right and proper that in bringing many sons to glory, God (from whom and by whom everything exists) should make the leader of their salvation a perfect leader through the fact that he suffered. For the one who makes men holy and the men who are made holy share a common humanity" (chapter 2:10, 11, *Phillips*).

But, who is He? Where did He come from? For Paul, Jesus the Man is the bench mark for humanity. He has shown men and women what humanity is like at its best.

Bible writers also make it clear that Jesus also showed us what God is like, that Jesus Christ is God in every respect. John declared: "The Word was God" (John 1:1). "And the Word became flesh and dwelt among us" (verse 14). Jesus stated His divine mission: "He who has seen me has seen the Father" (chapter 14:9). He recognized the successful completion of His mission: "I glorified thee on earth, having accomplished the work which thou gavest me to do; and now, Father, glorify thou me in thy own presence with the glory which I had with thee before the world was made" (chapter 17:4, 5).

If we are to answer that haunting question Jesus Christ, who are You? we must begin where the first Christians met Him and had to make their decision. They knew Him as a man who was totally involved in their common humanity. He was not a "reverse astronaut" who came to this world from "out of the blue" merely to tell us that God is alive and well, and that He loves us very much.

We can send men (and for that matter, women) to the moon, but they are still "earthmen"; they live within spacesuits that keep them untouched by the situation existing where they land. They live and eat, perform normal acts common to created beings, yet they are insulated from "life as it is" as they tramp around the moon.

No, Jesus was not an astronaut. As His early followers described Him (guided by His Spirit, whom He promised would help them to see, hear, and feel accurately when they wrote about Him), He became man without a protective spacesuit, either visible or invisible, that would separate Him from the kind of life lived by His contemporaries.

A very helpful Bible commentator described His identification with the human family on Planet Earth: "Jesus accepted humanity when the race had been weakened by four thousand years of sin. Like every child of Adam He accepted the results of the working of the great law of heredity. What these results were is shown in the history of His earthly ancestors. He came with such a heredity to share our sorrows and temptations, and to give us the example of a sinless life."[1]

Although He was born under the shadow of the Fall, taking humanity as any babe would find it 2,000 years ago—"with all its liabilities" (*ibid.,* p. 117)—He showed that men and women were not locked into a hopeless battle, that the shadow was not irrevocable, that sin was not inevitable, that God has always had a way out and up. He pulled the curtain back and showed all of us how to be truly human, the way God had meant for men and women to live.

Jesus Himself asked the big question one day in Caesarea Philippi, "But who do you say that I am?" And Peter shot back, with deep conviction, "You are the Christ, the Son of the living God" (Matthew 16:15, 16).

Those are spine-tingling words. Imagine eating and drinking, hiking and praying, with God! But they knew Him also to be man, truly man. God who became man! Incarnation!

Why? To reconcile sinners with God; to bridge earth's

---

[1] ELLEN G. WHITE, *The Desire of Ages* (Nampa, Idaho: Pacific Press Publishing Association [PPPA], 1940), p. 49.

Where Jesus Is Now

troubled waters with love and power! Paul described our Lord's marvelous mission: "For if while we were enemies we were reconciled to God by the death of his Son, much more, now that we are reconciled, shall we be saved by his life. Not only so, but we also rejoice in God through our Lord Jesus Christ, through whom we have now received our reconciliation" (Romans 5:10, 11).

Jesus Christ is the way back to Eden, the solution to human despair. He alone is the ground of mankind's hope and the only basis for man's redemption. See Him hanging between heaven and earth on Calvary's cross; the just suffering for the unjust, showing love for the unlovely! Measure your life by His! Claim His offer of pardon and full acceptance! Listen to His saving words, "I, when I am lifted up from the earth, will draw all men to myself" (John 12:32). "For God sent the Son into the world, not to condemn the world, but that the world might be saved through him" (chapter 3:17). Surely He is just what the angel promised and what I need—"a Savior, who is Christ the Lord" (Luke 2:11).

Another reason for our Lord's coming to earth and becoming truly man, "in every respect" (Hebrew 2:17), was to settle once and for all one of the basic questions of the great cosmic controversy—whether fallen men and women could live lives of happy obedience such as God had made provisions for.[2]

---

[2] "Satan has asserted that men could not keep the commandments of God. To prove that they could, Christ became a man, and lived a life of perfect obedience, an evidence to sinful human beings, to the world's unfallen, and to the heavenly angels, that man could keep God's law through the divine power that is abundantly provided for all that believe. In order to reveal God to the world, to demonstrate as true that which Satan has denied, Christ volunteered to take humanity, and in His power, humanity can obey God. . . . He was, as we are, subject to the enemy's temptations.

Jesus demolished the accusations of Satan that sin was inevitable and obedience impossible; that fallen humanity could not expect to live victoriously over sin. He demonstrated not only that men and women could keep God's law with the power provided but that God Himself was willing to risk the security of heaven in order to rescue men and women. He proved that there was nothing God asked *from* His creation that He was not willing to do *for* His creation. We do not need to go into an extended treatment of how Jesus became the eternal solution to the sin problem in order for our hearts to be drawn out in gratitude, praise, and adoration to God, who sent Jesus "as an expiation by his blood, to be received by faith" (Romans 3:25).

The death of Jesus "for us" (1 Thessalonians 5:10) is the focal point of time, the center of the plan of salvation, the prism through which the universe can see the full spectrum of God's love for His creation. The sacrifice of the Man Jesus proved God to be just, not unfair and capricious. It showed Him to be loving beyond human imagination. God proved that the violation of the basic laws of the universe have terrible consequences, which He demonstrated by allowing the "curse of the law" (Galatians 3:13) to be fully drained in Jesus' life and death.

Satan exulted when Christ became a human being, and he compassed His path with every conceivable temptation. Human weakness and tears were His portion; but He sought unto God, praying with His whole soul, with strong crying and tears; and He was heard in that He feared. The subtlety of the enemy could not ensnare Him while He made God His trust, and was obedient to His words. 'The prince of this world cometh,' He said, 'and hath nothing in Me.' He can find nothing in Me which responds to his sophistry."—ELLEN G. WHITE, *Signs of the Times,* May 10, 1899.

What an assignment God assumed by becoming man in Jesus! What a risk! But through His humanity, by becoming truly man, Jesus paid the price of man's folly and opened the door back to Eden.[3]

No wonder Ellen White sums up the adoration of our hearts when she wrote: "The humanity of the Son of God is everything to us. It is the golden chain that binds our souls to Christ, and through Christ to God. This is to be our study. Christ was a real man."[4]

One of the amazing aspects of God becoming man is that this gift was not temporary. *God became man forever!* "He [God] gave His only-begotten Son to come to earth, to take the nature of man, not only for the brief years of life, but to retain his nature in the heavenly courts, an everlasting pledge of the faithfulness of God."[5]

Contemplate the thought. It staggers the human mind.

---

[3] "Christ did not make believe take human nature; He did verily take it. He did in reality possess human nature. 'As the children are partakers of the flesh and blood, he also himself likewise took part of the same' (Heb. 2:14). He was the son of Mary; He was of the seed of David according to human descent. He is declared to be a man, even the Man Christ Jesus. . . .

"By His obedience to all the commandments of God, Christ wrought out a redemption for man. This was not done by going out of Himself to another, but by taking humanity into Himself. Thus Christ gave to humanity an existence out of Himself. To bring humanity into Christ, to bring the fallen race into oneness with divinity, is the work of redemption. Christ took human nature that men might be one with Him as He is one with the Father, that God may love man as He loves His only begotten Son, that men may be partakers of the divine nature, and be complete in Him."—ELLEN G. WHITE, *Review and Herald,* April 5, 1906.

[4] WHITE, *Selected Messages,* Bk. 1 (Washington, D.C.: Review and Herald Publishing Association [RHPA], 1958), p. 244.

[5] *Ibid.,* p. 258. See *The Desire of Ages,* p. 25.

We can understand somewhat the marvel of our Lord's birth in Bethlehem when He imprisoned Himself within His own creation. But for the Lord of Creation, who walked among the stars and whirled new universes into their orbits, to be forever cabined within time and space—this stretches the mind of men and women across unlimited oceans of love. Jesus truly *gave* Himself to Planet Earth and for you and me. God adopted human nature forever!

Men and women last saw Jesus on earth as they gathered on Mount Olivet shortly before He ascended into the sky and beyond their sight. But He left as they had known Him for 33 years—a human being such as themselves. As they watched, lost in wonder, "he was lifted up, and a cloud took him out of their sight" (Acts 1:9). Was He gone forever? Would those devoted followers ever see Him again? Where did He go?

Their questions were quickly dissolved with the angel's comforting statement: "Men of Galilee, why do you stand looking into heaven? This Jesus, who was taken up from you into heaven, will come in the same way as you saw him go into heaven" (verse 11).

Jesus, the Carpenter of Nazareth, the Friend of multitudes, the gracious Healer, *is now in heaven,* not as a disembodied spirit, not with the "form of God" that was His before He came to this earth (Philippians 2:6), but as man, retaining His human nature forever.

As such Stephen recognized Him when God graciously parted the veil between heaven and earth moments before his life was crushed out under the stones hurled by men who couldn't stand the truth. "But he, full of the Holy Spirit, gazed into heaven and saw the glory of God, and Jesus standing at the right hand of God; and he said, 'Behold, I see the heavens opened, and the Son of man standing at the right hand of God' " (Acts 7:55, 56).

Paul heard His voice on that fateful day on the Damascus road. In the midst of Paul's spiritual banditry Jesus stepped into his life with the breathtaking question: " 'Saul, Saul, why do you persecute me?' And he said, 'Who are you, Lord?' And he said, 'I am Jesus, whom you are persecuting' " (chapter 9:4, 5).

John was given an awesome glimpse of his Master while he was exiled on rocky Patmos. Wasn't that a gracious gesture on our Lord's part—to give His old friend, who had witnessed gloriously to His cause, the final assurance that all was not in vain! "When I saw him, I fell at his feet as though dead. But he laid his right hand upon me, saying, 'Fear not, I am the first and the last, and the living one; I died, and behold I am alive for evermore, and I have the keys of Death and Hades' " (Revelation 1:17, 18).

But as time went on something very curious and sad happened to the Christian church. They lost sight of where Jesus *now* is and what He is *now* doing on our behalf. Over the centuries many in the church fixed their attention on Him dying on the cross—the personification of human tragedy. They have exalted Jesus as the greatest teacher of righteousness mankind has ever heard, honored Him for untainted integrity in full blossom, revered Him for the moral impulse He has injected into human history. They are moved by the utter abandonment to His ideals that drove Him to the cross rather than flinch or concede to evil. But that is where they last see Him—on the cross.

Other Christians went further; they fixed their attention on Jesus as the resurrected Saviour. They saw

Him mingle with His followers for forty days and then marvelously ascend to heaven. But somehow they lost Him in the vagueness of light-years and theological jargon regarding the atonement. Although they know that He is in heaven "at the right hand of God" they have no clear-cut understanding of Christ's continuing role in the working out of the plan of salvation.

To see Him only on the cross is seeing only in part; glorious, but only in part. To see Him only as the resurrected Lord is also seeing Him in part. Appealing and winsome is this beautiful picture of love unlimited—God paying the price for a fallen race, and rising triumphantly from the grave—a dual demonstration of love and power. But a partial picture of Jesus leads to important misunderstandings, such as believing that His love is irresistible and that someday in God's good time all men and women will be convinced and thus won back to a reunited kingdom of grace and love. Or, that simple gratefulness in recognizing that He died for everyone's sin is in itself the test of a person's fitness to be saved.

Seventh-day Adventists believe that there is more to our Lord's role in the plan of salvation than to see Him only on the cross, wonderful and indispensable as His death was. Or even to see Him as our resurrected Lord, glorious in all of its implications. They follow Jesus into the heavenly sanctuary, they fix their eyes on Him, the Great High Priest of the human family, the living hope of everyone who seeks pardon and victory over the forces of sin.

Throughout the book of Hebrews Paul sings the glorious song of our Lord's continuing ministry for fallen men and women. For example: "Since then we have a great high priest who has passed through the heavens,

Jesus, the Son of God, let us hold fast our confession" (Hebrews 4:14).

Paul declares that a clear understanding of Jesus as our High Priest is "a sure and steadfast anchor of the soul, a hope that enters into the inner shrine behind the curtain, where Jesus has gone as a forerunner on our behalf" (chapter 6:19, 20). He proclaimed that Christians can boldly enter "the sanctuary by the blood of Jesus, by the new and living way which he opened for us through the curtain, that is, through his flesh, and since we have a great priest over the house of God, let us draw near with a true heart, in full assurance of faith, with our hearts sprinkled clean from an evil conscience and our bodies washed with pure water" (chapter 10:19-22).

Something very significant to the plan of salvation is going on in heaven today because Jesus is our High Priest. Something significant and special should be going on in the lives of His followers on earth because of Jesus' role as our High Priest, as we will study in the pages to come.

Following Jesus into the heavenly sanctuary does not depreciate the Cross. God forbid. Without the Cross there would have been no High Priest in the heavenly sanctuary today. But what Jesus is now doing is probably the most important subject to be understood by those on planet Earth.[6]

Our concern for ecological imbalances, for population explosions, for the proliferation of nuclear weaponry, for waste disposal—for whatever, all such concerns fade into insignificance compared with what we should

---

[6] "The intercession of Christ in man's behalf in the sanctuary above is as essential to the plan of salvation as was His death upon the cross."—WHITE, *The Great Controversy* (Nampa, Idaho: PPPA, 1948), p. 489.

know about Jesus and what He is trying to do for this shuddering planet. Where Jesus is now, and what He wants to do, must be understood by all who seek lasting peace in their heart and a part in hastening the return of their Lord.

No wonder Ellen White wrote, "God's people are now to have their eyes fixed on the heavenly sanctuary, where the final ministration of our great High Priest in the work of the judgment is going forward—where He is interceding for His people."[7]

Easily we can understand why Paul urged his readers: "For we have not a high priest who is unable to sympathize with our weaknesses, but one who in every respect has been tempted as we are, yet without sinning. Let us then with confidence draw near to the throne of grace, that we may receive mercy [pardon] and find grace [power] to help in time of need."—Hebrews 4:15, 16.

In the following pages we will follow our Lord into the sanctuary[8] of the universe, see Him in His role as Sacrifice and Priest for all who claim Him as Lord, and listen to Him as He invites us to cooperate with Him in completing His grand rescue plan for sinners on planet Earth.

---

[7] WHITE, *Evangelism* (Washington, D.C.: RHPA, 1946), p. 223.

[8] The term "the sanctuary" has been appropriately applied over the years by Seventh-day Adventists to the Old Testament earthly tabernacle (and, by implication, its service), to the heavenly antitypical sanctuary (and its service), to the Christian church, and to the committed Christian who permits himself to become an abode for the God of heaven, who delights to dwell "with him who is of a contrite and humble spirit" (Isaiah 57:15). Each definition will be examined in pages to come.

Importance of the Sanctuary Truth

WHAT IS so distinctive about the sanctuary doctrine that makes Seventh-day Adventism unique in the theological world?[1]

Why is it said that giving up the sanctuary truth is virtually declaring oneself no longer to be a Seventh-day Adventist?

Let it be said simply and clearly: The biblical doctrine of the sanctuary, as set forth by the Seventh-day Adventist Church, is the center of gravity for the plan of salvation, the hub of the theological wheel, which explains and connects all the biblical truths that Christians hold dear, especially those truths that have been overlooked for centuries.

Ellen G. White, one of the long-time leaders of the Adventist Church, wrote that the sanctuary doctrine "opened to view a complete system of truth, connected and harmonious, showing that God's hand had directed

---

[1] "The correct understanding of the ministration in the heavenly sanctuary is the foundation of our faith."—WHITE, *Evangelism*, p. 221.

the great advent movement and revealing present duty as it brought to light the position and work of His people."[2]

Many Adventist scholars have placed similar emphasis on the sanctuary doctrine. Stephen N. Haskell, author of *The Cross and Its Shadow,* noted that "we cannot overestimate the importance of the sanctuary question. . . . It is by this subject that we obtain a clear insight into the mysteries of redemption. . . . It is *His work alone in heaven,* made manifest in the lives of His people on earth, that connects any soul with God. . . . The sanctuary question was to reveal Christ, His work in the heavenly courts, and as it would be carried on in the hearts of His disciples. It is thus apparent that the work in the hearts of the people must correspond with that of Christ in heaven. . . .

"All the work revealed by the typical temple shadowing the real work of Christ in heaven is for the purification of His Church on the earth, and consequently a neglect of a knowledge of these truths will leave men unprepared for the impending judgments of God, as really as the Jews were unprepared for the destruction that came upon them."[3]

The doctrine of the sanctuary, therefore, is not an elective subject, reserved for advanced Bible students, or for those who happen to be interested in the exotic and mysterious. It is for every believer. It is not a theme that can be understood completely or even properly understood in part, by intellectual re-

---

[2] WHITE, *The Great Controversy,* p. 423.

[3] "The Sanctuary Question From the Standpoint of the Book of Hebrews," *Review and Herald,* Aug. 13, 1901.

search alone. To understand fully, one must also experience the truth the sanctuary doctrine is describing.[4]

W. W. Prescott, Adventist thought leader and editor of the Church's world paper (1901–1909), wrote extensively on the relationship of the sanctuary doctrine and the distinctive mission of the Adventist Church. In a sermon presented at the 1903 General Conference session he said, "There is something in these different steps in the development of God's purpose of salvation from sin as set forth in the sanctuary and its services that makes a difference to the people of God, that they ought to know. It is God's purpose that they should know this, and it is necessary for them to know it, in order to cooperate intelligently

---

[4] "We are in the day of atonement, and we are to work in harmony with Christ's work of cleansing the sanctuary from the sins of the people. Let no man who desires to be found with the wedding garment on, resist our Lord in his office work. As He is, so will His followers be in this world. We must now set before the people the work which by faith we see our great High-priest accomplishing in the heavenly sanctuary. Those who do not sympathize with Jesus in His work in the heavenly courts, who do not cleanse the soul temple of every defilement, but who engage in some enterprise not in harmony with this work, are joining with the enemy of God and man in leading minds away from the truth and work for this time. . . .

"The work in the heavenly sanctuary becomes obscure to the minds of those who are controlled by the temptations of the evil one, and they engage in side issues to gratify their own selfish purposes, and their true moral standing is determined by their works. . . .

"It is Satan's studied effort to make of none effect saving, testing truth through the lives of those who preach the truth to others and who in their daily practices deny what they preach."—WHITE, *Review and Herald,* January 21, 1890.

with the development of God's purpose of salvation as found in this question."⁵

In a series of articles in the *Review and Herald* during the pantheism crisis, Prescott tried to sort out the differences between those who contended that all men were living temples of God's presence and those who believed that only the converted were God's temples. Understanding the differences depended upon the right understanding of the sanctuary doctrine and the subject of righteousness by faith.

He declared that "the heart of the sanctuary question is found in the great truth that it is God's purpose to dwell with flesh. . . .

"It is plain enough that when Christ our righteousness dwells in the heart by faith, making the flesh his temple, we have the actual experience of righteousness by faith. It follows then that the central thought in the sanctuary question is righteousness by faith, or justification by faith."⁶

The sanctuary doctrine is God's way of picturing the plan of salvation—both His part and ours. The sanctuary service, as unfolded to the Israelites in their wilderness experience and more fully explained in the New Testament, was not intended to obscure the plan of salvation, but to make it simple and appealing. It seems necessary to make this point because for so many the subject of the sanctuary has been strange and uninteresting.

When the sanctuary truth is properly understood it removes mysteries rather than creates them. When seen

---

[5] "The Gospel Message for Today," *General Conference Bulletin*, April 2, 1903, p. 52.

[6] "Studies in the Gospel Message," *Review and Herald*, July 15, 1902, p. 6.

in its New Testament setting the sanctuary doctrine loses its shadows and clarifies the truth about the roles that both God and man play in the grand and glorious plan of salvation—even as the noonday sun brightens dark paths and highlights the colors of the geranium or rose.

So the question remains: Why is the sanctuary service as a Christian doctrine such a mystery to many Seventh-day Adventists, to say nothing of those who have not had the Seventh-day Adventist experience? Why is it, for so many, a difficult, complex, and often uninteresting hurdle in the chain of Bible studies a non-Seventh-day Adventist takes before baptism, and rarely studies afterward?

Perhaps because the emphasis has often been on the shadows of the Old Testament picture rather than on the noonday sun of the New Testament explanation. Perhaps because the sanctuary doctrine has been considered more as a subject to be learned than a truth to be experienced. Perhaps because elementary details are repeated over and over again, leaving the impression that there is really nothing more to learn.

For instance, treating the sanctuary doctrine as most Protestant or Catholic systematic theologians or expositors do, gives the student nothing distinctive to captivate his thoughts. Merely to intone the words that Jesus is our High Priest—that He intercedes day and night for His people, that His sacrifice on the cross "paid the price" of our redemption, that He provides pardon for the daily sins of His people—is not enough. These great truths are fundamental in understanding the biblical truth regarding the heavenly sanctuary and the function of our Lord as High Priest. But such observations, glorious as they are, do not constitute the whole story. Thus they tend to mislead.

Liberal theologians tend to discard the supernatural and thus end their concern for our Lord's role in the plan of salvation on the cross. They see Him as a great teacher dying for His cause, a brilliant human display of divine attributes. But, for them, there is no high-priestly role, no heavenly sanctuary, no judgment to come, no Second Advent.

Conservative theologians, though affirming our Lord's supernatural pre-existence and His supernatural ascension and exaltation, also tend, for practical purposes, to focus almost exclusively on His death. Very little exists, in even extensive studies on the work of Jesus Christ, regarding the place, purpose, and function of His high-priestly role, except that He is in heaven, seated at the right hand of God, interceding through the prayers He offers for His people. To focus on our Lord's death while eclipsing His high-priestly role and its effect on His followers on earth is to misunderstand the plan of redemption.

Therefore, to study and restudy some of the truths without seeing the whole picture would be just what the evil one would order. In such circumstances, instead of gripping the whole person experientially, partial truths become only facts to be learned. When these facts are presented often, the eager hearer finds himself strangely bored as the speaker or writer belabors the obvious. Something sets in akin to the boredom and disinterest of the eager schoolboy who already knows his basic arithmetic but must endure the daily exercises of those who are still catching up. Nothing is more disenchanting than reviewing the obvious. It is

Importance of the Sanctuary Truth

worse yet, however, for the student to get the idea that knowing how to add and subtract is all there is to the world of mathematics, and that those who use these numbers in a language called algebra are indulging in purely personal speculation.

God never intended that the sanctuary doctrine should create boredom, indifference, or even mystery.[7] Not the God who impressed the psalmist to write, "Thy way, O God, is in the sanctuary: who is so great a God as our God" (Psalm 77:13, KJV)?

The Israelite in the wilderness could lift his eyes and see the smoke of the daily sacrifices rising toward heaven and the awesome light of God's presence gloriously bathing the Most Holy Place. For him the sanctuary was not a boring subject. It was the center of his life.

For the Christian, what the sanctuary doctrine teaches about Jesus must also be the center of his experience, the heart of his faith, the living, throbbing theological muscle that makes faith, hope, and love possible.

Whenever Christians, for whatever reason, become spiritually anemic, and life itself becomes dreary, laden with guilt and despair, and enshrouded in foggy meaninglessness, spiritual recovery will be hastened as they

---

[7] For an example of Adventist concern regarding the decline of interest in the sanctuary doctrine, observations such as the following are typical: "Some may feel that the sanctuary truth was relevant 131 years ago, but that it is outmoded today. Probably that is why there has been an apparent decline in interest in and study of the sanctuary in recent times. But the sanctuary and its services must always have meaning and significance for Seventh-day Adventists."—J. A. McMillan, "Is the Sanctuary Truth Relevant Today?" *Review and Herald,* June 5, 1975, p. 10.

refresh themselves with the truths of the sanctuary doctrine. I assure you!

What are these truths wrapped up in the sanctuary that remove the weight of the past, give power to the present, and hope for the future?

Simply these, thank God! The sanctuary doctrine makes clear what God has done *for us* and what He wants to do *in us*.[8] He not only made provision to forgive and cancel our sins; He Himself paid the price of this reconciliation through the life and death of our Lord Jesus Christ. More than that, He extends to all who accept His provisions the grace and power that kept Jesus from sinning so that He will have a people who are truly cleansed, an eternal memorial to love and grace. These glorious truths we will explore in the following pages.

"For Christ has entered, not into a sanctuary made with hands, a copy of the true one, but into heaven itself, now to appear in the presence of God on our behalf" (Hebrews 9:24).

---

[8] The clearest statement I have ever read that sums up God's role in man's salvation is "Our only ground of hope is in the righteousness of Christ imputed to us, and in that wrought by His Spirit working in and through us."—WHITE, *Steps to Christ* (Washington, D.C.: RHPA, 1908), p. 63. Here the ellipse of truth is clearly demonstrated. See footnote No. 6 on page 37.

The Historical Anchor

ONE OF the reasons for the importance of the sanctuary doctrine is that it anchors the historical basis for the message and mission of the Seventh-day Adventist Church: "The subject of the sanctuary was the key which unlocked the mystery of the disappointment of 1844."[1] In fact, Ellen White further declared, "The scripture which above all others had been both the foundation and the central pillar of the advent faith was the declaration: 'Unto two thousand and three hundred days; then shall the sanctuary be cleansed.' Daniel 8:14."[2]

If the sanctuary doctrine is "the very message that has made us a separate people, and has given character and power to our work,"[3] then we must know the reasons for this. Or else we will drift into that dreamy sea where we sense no specific urgency or distinctiveness as a people. Our reason for existence as a church would be blurred indeed if we should forget the unique implications of the sanctuary doctrine.

---

[1] WHITE, *The Great Controversy*, p. 423.
[2] *Ibid.*, p. 409.
[3] WHITE, *Evangelism*, p. 225.

As early as 1851 Ellen White and others saw clearly that "such subjects as the sanctuary, in connection with the 2300 days, the commandments of God and the faith of Jesus, are perfectly calculated to explain the past Advent movement and show what our present position is, establish the faith of the doubting, and give certainty to the glorious future. These, I have frequently seen, were the principal subjects on which the messengers should dwell."[4]

The sanctuary doctrine anchored the Seventh-day Adventist Church in history and gave it purpose in existence, because it explained the significance of October 22, 1844. Although many thousands of Millerite Adventists turned away from the rich experience that bound them to one another and to their Lord after the day of Great Disappointment, others did not repudiate the validity of their experience; these continued to study the Bible, endeavoring to understand more clearly the meaning of Daniel 8:14.

William Miller had based his electrifying message that Jesus would return to this earth about 1843/1844 primarily on Daniel 8:14.[5] He first declared the church to be the sanctuary that was to be cleansed. Later he stated it to be the church and the earth, both of which would be cleansed by the fires of the last day at the close of the 2300-year prophecy.

After an adjustment was made in Miller's chronol-

---

[4] WHITE, *Early Writings* (Washington, D.C.: RHPA, 1945), p. 63.

[5] For a short study of the 2300-day/year prophecy, beginning in 457 B.C., see *The Great Controversy,* pages 409, 410; for the historical basis that establishes the validity and significance of the date 457 B.C., see SIEGFRIED H. HORN, and LYNN H. WOOD, *The Chronology of Ezra 7* (Washington, DC: RHPA, 1970), and *The SDA Bible Commentary,* vol. 3, pp. 85–110.

THE HISTORICAL ANCHOR

ogy, to better conform to the Karaite reckoning of the Israelite calendar, the Millerites changed the expectation of the Second Advent from the spring of 1844 to the fall, on October 22.[6]

During the spring and summer of 1844 closer study was given to the sanctuary doctrine and its application to the Christian gospel. That Christ was to come out of the Most Holy Place on the antitypical day of atonement at the time of His second advent became clearer. *But it was not seen* that the concept that Jesus would leave the Most Holy Place—a part of the heavenly sanctuary—to "cleanse" by fire the so-called sanctuary on earth at His second advent in 1844, was in error.

Steps toward resolving the confusion that called both the earth and heaven the sanctuary referred to in Daniel 8:14 were taken the day after the Great Disappointment. Two Millerites, Hiram Edson and a friend, were deep in contemplation while crossing a farmer's field near Port Gibson, New York, to visit a group of disheartened Millerite Adventists. Edson suddenly saw the paradox and perceived that "instead of our High Priest coming out of the Most Holy of the heavenly sanctuary to come to this earth on the tenth day of the seventh month, at the end of the 2300 days, . . . He for the first time entered on that day the second apartment of that sanctuary; and

---

[6] "Through study of Babylonian astronomical and mathematical data, it is now possible to arrive at the precise date for the Day of Atonement in 457 B.C. and by mathematical calculation to establish the modern equivalent for this date in 1844."—RICHARD M. DAVIDSON, in "Confirmation of the Sanctuary Message," *Journal of the Adventist Theological Society,* 2/1 (1991), pp. 93–114. See also WILLIAM H. SHEA, "Day of Atonement and October 22, 1844," *Selected Studies on Prophetic Interpretation* (Washington, D.C.: RHPA, 1982), pp. 132–137.

that He had a work to perform in the Most Holy before coming to this earth."[7]

For several months Hiram Edson, Owen R. L. Crosier, and Franklin B. Hahn studied anew the sanctuary doctrine. Crosier published preliminary results of these studies in 1845 and more expanded discourses in 1846-1847. In these articles and letters it was forcefully stated that the heavenly sanctuary was the only sanctuary existing when the 2300-year prophecy ended in 1844; thus, it was the only sanctuary to be cleansed at that time.

Crosier's view, which also represented those of Hahn and Edson, was quickly accepted by James White and Joseph Bates. This particular concept was endorsed by Ellen White as "the true light, on the cleansing of the Sanctuary, &c."[8]

Crosier's position provided a base for those Adventists who would not reject their "experience" of the 1844 disappointment by blindly declaring that the 1844 computation was in error, or accept the explanation of the "spiritualizers" who held to the prophetical correctness of 1844 but reinterpreted the event as the "coming of Jesus" into the lives of faithful Christians. For those who stood with Crosier, the heavenly sanctuary was as literal as was the New Jerusalem. For them the event marked by the end of the 2300 years of Daniel 8:14 was the transition in Christ's high-priestly ministry from the Holy Place in the heavenly sanctuary to the Most Holy Place, signifying a new and final work on behalf of His people.

---

[7] Don F. Neufeld, ed., *Seventh-day Adventist Encyclopedia* (Washington, DC: RHPA, 1976) p. 1142, for this portion of Hiram Edson's manuscript entitled "Life and Experience."

[8] *Ibid.*

The Historical Anchor

In addition, Crosier declared that "there is a literal and a spiritual temple—the literal being the Sanctuary in the New Jerusalem (literal city), and the spiritual the church—the literal occupied by Jesus Christ, our King and Priest . . .; the spiritual by the Holy Ghost. . . . Between these two there is a perfect concert of action, as Christ 'prepares the *place*' the Spirit does the people. When He came to His temple, the sanctuary, to cleanse it; the Spirit commenced the special cleansing of the people. Mal. 3:1-3."[9]

Crosier's presentation on this point became the nucleus for the standard position taken by Seventh-day Adventists. But there was much yet to follow as the sanctuary doctrine was more fully studied. The concept of the judgment, especially the investigative, or pre-Advent,[10] phase, was not yet linked with Crosier's clarification regarding the cleansing of the heavenly sanctuary and the judgment-hour message of Revelation 14.

During this period, after Crosier's study settled the location of the sanctuary referred to in Daniel 8:14, other Bible references to the heavenly sanctuary became clearer. The revelator's depiction (Revelation 11: 19) of events during the seventh trumpet became very relevant, especially the reference to the heavenly sanctuary: "The temple of God was opened in heaven, and there was seen in his temple the ark of his testament" (KJV). It is the truth contained in these words, developed by other portions of Scripture, that formed the historical and

---

[9] Letter (March 31, 1846), printed in *The Day-Star,* April 18, 1846, p. 31.

[10] A phrase that was used, possibly for the first time, by EDWARD HEPPENSTALL, *Our High Priest* (Washington, D.C.: RHPA, 1972), p. 107.

theological uniqueness of the Seventh-day Adventist Church.[11]

Understanding the sanctuary doctrine led Adventists to see the importance of the biblical Sabbath, the seventh day of the week. Accepting the truth of the heavenly sanctuary as anchored in the 1844 experience "involved an acknowledgment of the claims of God's law and the obligation of the Sabbath of the fourth commandment."[12]

Not before J. N. Loughborough's article in 1854[13] was the cleansing of the sanctuary linked with the judgment-hour message as set forth in the first angel's message of Revelation 14. Not until James White's *Review* article in 1857[14] were the concepts of the in-

---

[11] "They [early Seventh-day Adventists] found that at a certain time, under the sounding of the seventh angel, Christ would change His position in the heavenly sanctuary from the holy to the most holy place; and this was the event which they had concluded would take place in 1844. This discovery of their mistake was not made until the time had passed. They then saw by faith the inner sanctuary in heaven, and the commandments in the ark of the testament; and it was the study of this sanctuary question, and the truths connected with it, which led a people to keep the commandments of God, and to be separate, as the Seventh-day Adventists are at the present time."—STEPHEN N. HASKELL, "Bible Study," *General Conference Bulletin,* April 7, 1901, pp. 98, 99.

[12] WHITE, *The Great Controversy,* p. 435.

[13] "The Hour of His Judgment Come," *Review and Herald,* Feb. 14, 1854, pp. 29, 30.

[14] White concluded from such texts as 1 Peter 4:17, 18, that only two classes are recognized in the judgment, that "each class has its time of judgment; and, according to the text, the judgment of the house, or church, of God comes first in order.

"Both classes will be judged before they are raised from the dead. The investigative judgment of the house, or church, of God will take place before the first resurrection; so will the judgment of the wicked take place during the 1000 years of Rev. xx, and they will be raised at

vestigative judgment, the cleansing of the sanctuary, and the judgment-hour message joined and settled permanently in Seventh-day Adventist thought.

Thus, a group of post-1844 Adventists moved from one biblical link to the next: from (1) determining the heavenly sanctuary as that referred to in Daniel 8:14, to (2) understanding the Most Holy Place of that sanctuary to be the place of Christ's new role as High Priest since 1844, to (3) the acknowledgment that obeying God's law in its fullness was inextricably connected with the new light on the sanctuary doctrine, to (4) the awareness that the distinctive truths enunciated in the messages of the three angels of Revelation 14 coincided with their enlarging cluster of sanctuary truths. The 1844 date historically anchored the doctrine of the investigative, or pre-Advent, judgment and the beginning of the judgment hour announced by the first angel in Revelation 14.

The link between the maturing doctrine of the sanctuary and the messages of the three angels of Revelation 14 gave new impetus to the young band of Adventists who were now Sabbath keepers.[15]

---

the close of that period."—"The Judgment," *Review and Herald*, Jan. 29, 1857, p. 100.

[15] In 1850, James White wrote: "A part of the third angel's message is—'Here is the patience of the saints; here are they that keep the commandments of God,' &c. [Rev. 14:12]. We know that the saints' patient waiting time has been since their disappointment in 1844.—Well here it is, and we all know it. We cannot be mistaken here. We know then that the time for this third message is now. We know also that the time for keeping all the commandments right has been since 1844, since God called us out of Babylon. . . .

" 'And the temple of God was opened in heaven, and there was seen in his temple the ark of his testament.' Rev. xi, 19. Did John see the ark of the ten commandments in heaven? Yes, so he testifies; and

The members of the growing Adventist movement sensed the urgency implicit in living in the judgment hour, when the life records of all the righteous of this earth, the dead and then the living, would be judged in the heavenly tribunal. They had experienced the excitement of preaching the message of the first angel prior to 1844; some believed, further, that they were sounding the call of the second angel during the summer of 1844, "Babylon is fallen," when many of them were expelled from their own churches. And now, with their new insight into the coordinated sequence of the three messages, plus their awareness of the third angel's emphatic warning against worshiping "the beast and its image" and the commendation for those who "keep the commandments of God, and the faith of Jesus"—the basic platform for the emerging church was formed.

Seventh-day Adventists saw in the sanctuary doctrine "a complete system of truth, connected and harmonious, showing that God's hand had directed the great

---

none who believe the Bible will doubt his testimony, and say that he some how fell into a mesmeric state, and saw things incorrectly. Then if the commandments are preserved in heaven, certainly they are not abolished on earth.

"In the type, the temple of God on earth, the place for the ark was in the 'holiest of all,' within the second veil. In the antitype, 'the temple of God' 'in heaven,' the ark must be in the same place, for the earthly were *'patterns of things in the heavens.'* In the earthly, 'the holiest of all' was opened at the end of the year, for the high priest alone to enter on the day that he cleansed the sanctuary; but the 'holiest of all' of the heavenly 'temple' was not opened until Jesus, our High Priest, entered to cleanse the sanctuary at the end of the 2300 days, in 1844. . . .

"God has marked out our past experience and present position so very clearly, that none need doubt. All the saints may see and know their whereabouts, and understand present truth and present duty."— "The Third Angel's Message," *The Present Truth,* April, 1850.

advent movement and revealing present duty as it brought to light the position and work of His people."[16] They saw clearly the validity of the 1844 experience, crushing as it was before its meaning became clear. They saw their present duty as spokesmen for God in sounding the dire warnings and divine invitation of the third angel of Revelation 14 to all who would listen. They saw the future in the light of God's judgment on this earth, life for the righteous and destruction for the wicked.

Past, present, future—all became clearer because of the sanctuary doctrine. What this expanding understanding of the sanctuary doctrine meant experientially to Adventists in the mid-nineteenth century and what it should mean to us today will now be studied.[17]

---

[16] WHITE, *The Great Controversy,* p. 423.

[17] Stephen N. Haskell expressed it well: "If your faith is not revived in the sanctuary question and in the work of our High Priest, and if you do not get an experience out of it, I fear you will never go through. We must have an experience in this work of our High Priest."— Sermon preached at College View, Nebraska (1904), printed in MATTIE H. WELCH, *Present Truth for Perilous Times* (Nashville, Tenn: Southern Publishing Association, n.d.).

The Truth Satan Fears Most

COUNSEL HAS been given that "the subject of the sanctuary and the investigative judgment should be clearly understood by the people of God."[1] This knowledge is to be more than a textbook understanding. Without it the church member will eventually lose his soul, as Ellen White further declares: "All need a knowledge for themselves of the position and work of their great High Priest. Otherwise it will be impossible for them to exercise the faith which is essential at this time or to occupy the position which God designs them to fill."[2] Such a dire warning has been given by Ellen White about no other biblical subject!

Why is Ellen White so emphatic? What is there about the sanctuary doctrine that is so fundamental to a correct understanding of the message and mission of the Seventh-day Adventist Church? Furthermore, why is there such silence in the Christian church generally, and Adventist pulpits in particular, regarding the doc-

---

[1] White, *The Great Controversy*, p. 488.
[2] *Ibid.*

trine? And why such a strange boredom among Adventists regarding the sanctuary truths if they are so vital to the spiritual health of each church member, especially in these days since 1844? Simply because Satan does not want the towering truths about Jesus, which are embodied in the sanctuary doctrine, to be understood. He doesn't mind if church members pay their tithe, recognize the Sabbath as God's holy day, and build larger schools and hospitals. He is not too troubled if church members pray daily for Jesus to forgive their sins and for Him to return soon to this earth. After all, people who did similarly once crucified Jesus.

But Satan does hate "the great truths that bring to view an atoning sacrifice and an all-powerful mediator. He knows that with him everything depends on his diverting minds from Jesus and His truth."[3] Consequently, "Satan invents unnumbered schemes to occupy our minds, that they may not dwell upon the very work with which we ought to be best acquainted."[4]

In other words, if Satan can cause confusion or boredom with two central truths in the plan of salvation, he cares not how much else we may know or do. These central truths are (1) the "atoning sacrifice" and (2) the "all-powerful mediator." In these are linked indissolubly what Jesus has done *for us* and what He wants to do *in us*.[5]

---

[3] *Ibid.*

[4] *Ibid.*

[5] "Our only ground of hope is in the righteousness of Christ imputed to us, and in that wrought by His Spirit working in and through us."—WHITE, *Steps to Christ,* p. 63.

A major, and perennial, problem of Christianity is that men and women tend to focus on either what Jesus has done or what He wants to do in us. Rarely are these two concepts held in proper relationship as two foci in an ellipse.[6] When the atoning sacrifice, what Jesus has done *for us,* is featured disproportionately, too often the record shows that the work of the Holy Spirit is slighted; a cold, rigid, doctrine-oriented religion often develops. Often, in reaction to this overemphasis, the work of the all-powerful Mediator becomes overstressed by equally earnest Christians who sense the void in their personal experience caused by an overly intellectualized religion. But unduly emphasizing what Christ does *in us* focuses disproportionate attention on the hearer and his religious experience; the historic Word and the objective atonement of our Lord are not properly emphasized and are thus obscured. Faith then becomes more a matter of feeling and a reflection of a person's religious experi-

---

[6] To emphasize only one focal point in an ellipse is to distort the ellipse. In doing so, the ellipse becomes two circles, one outshadowing the other. All the divisions between various churches within Christianity, and between Christianity and other world religions, occur when the ellipse of truth is ignored. When one of the foci becomes the "circle of truth," we have a heresy (a partial truth that becomes a whole error). Even though each focal point in the ellipse emphasizes truth worth dying for, arguments will never end until a person accepts the total picture of the truths emphasized in both foci. This understanding of truth is as inescapable as the joining of hydrogen and oxygen to make water. It is the wrong question to ask, Which is more important, hydrogen or oxygen? So, it is the wrong question to ask, Which is more important, what Jesus did on the cross or what Jesus is now doing as our High Priest. For a discussion of the "ellipse of salvation truth," see HERBERT E. DOUGLASS, *Messenger of the Lord* (Nampa, Idaho: PPPA, 1998), p. 573.

ence than an obedient response to God, our Creator and Redeemer.

An understanding of the basic truths of the sanctuary doctrine will rescue church members from these twin errors of overconfident intellectual security on the one hand, and overconfident emotionalism on the other. The sanctuary truths will save us from being caught in the futile battle of slogans, which, in themselves, express only half-truths when improperly stressed. For instance, when not correctly understood, those who cry, "Not of works, lest any man should boast," must also be prepared for the counterthrust, "Not of creed, lest any man should boast of that."

Both errors bypass the real intent of the plan of salvation—the eradication of sinful habits in the Christian's life, here and now. The sanctuary doctrine properly understood will help bring the truths that reside in both over-emphases into a harmonious concept of the plan of salvation.[7]

---

[7] W. W. Prescott recognized this perennial danger of falling into one or the other error that springs out of misunderstanding how God wants to help men and women destroy sin. For the Seventh-day Adventist Church—especially in his day—the subtle temptation had been to find security in doctrinal belief and visible loyalty to such divine requirements as the seventh-day Sabbath and health reform.

At the General Conference in 1903 he declared: "Now that preaching of Christ, and Him crucified, that preaching of the righteousness of Christ as the gift of God through faith in Jesus, which does not extend to and take in these definite developments of advent history, of advent experience, and these definite developments of the truth for this generation, is not the preaching of righteousness by faith, or Christ crucified, that God would have preached to the people now.

THE TRUTH SATAN FEARS MOST

What Satan fears most is that some generation will take God seriously and listen to Him carefully.[8] Satan

---

"Now do not misunderstand me. I will speak in the plainest manner. You know I am not preaching against the forgiveness of sin, the righteousness of Christ, and the glory of the cross of Christ. But what I want to emphasize is this, that not by going off on one side, and ignoring all the historic truth, and all the prophetic truth, and simply preaching a general message of salvation through faith in Christ, without applying God's message of salvation through faith in Christ *to this generation,* is not the preaching that God wants in this generation. (Congregation, 'Amen.') The preaching of the glory of the cross of Christ, the preaching of the light that shines from Calvary's cross, the preaching of the righteousness of Christ as our only hope of salvation, must in this generation extend to a definite application and enforcement of these truths, in the light of advent history and advent prophecy. And when those truths are preached in the light of advent history and advent prophecy they will save people from sin and from sinning now. They will prepare a people to stand in the hour of temptation that faces us, and will prepare a people to meet the Lord in the air, and so to be ever with the Lord; and that is the message to be preached in this generation."—"The Gospel Message for Today," *General Conference Bulletin,* April 2, 1903, p. 54.

[8] "Satan invents unnumbered schemes to occupy our minds, that they may not dwell upon the very work with which we ought to be best acquainted. The archdeceiver hates the great truths that bring to view an atoning sacrifice and an all-powerful mediator. He knows that with him everything depends on his diverting minds from Jesus and His truth.

"Those who would share the benefits of the Saviour's mediation should permit nothing to interfere with their duty to perfect holiness in the fear of God. The precious hours, instead of being given to pleasure, to display, or to gain seeking, should be devoted to an earnest, prayerful study of the word of truth. The subject of the sanctuary and the investigative judgment should be clearly understood by the people of God. All need a knowledge for themselves of the position and work of their great High Priest. Otherwise it will be impossible for them to exercise the faith which is essential at this time or to occupy the position which God designs them to fill."— WHITE, *The Great Controversy,* p. 488.

fears that Seventh-day Adventists will take God at His word and cooperate with Him in the eradication of sinful habits and thus become indeed faithful witnesses to the power of the gospel (Matt. 24:14). Satan fears that Adventists will join their concern for commandment keeping with the "faith of Jesus" (Revelation 14:12). Satan fears that those who sincerely desire the "faith of Jesus" will also develop the character of Jesus. Satan fears that those who develop the character of Jesus through faith in God's abiding power will prove him wrong before the observing universe.

Satan fears that once-fettered men and women, each one with a past record of selfishness and spiritual failure, will demonstrate that God's way of life is the happiest, nicest, healthiest way to live. Satan fears that this winsome, appealing character of such commandment keepers will hasten the Advent and his final destruction, for "Christ is waiting with longing desire for the manifestation of Himself in His church. When the character of Christ shall be perfectly reproduced in His people, then He will come to claim them as His own."[9]

Satan fears that these glorious possibilities will be uncovered when men and women study the sanctuary doctrine. He will even be satisfied if church members fix their eyes on the cross where their Lord hangs between heaven and earth—as long as they do not follow Him into the heavenly sanctuary and discover why He lived and died as He did. Satan will be satisfied if church members pour out their offerings in ever-increasing percentages, build the nicest educational and medical insti-

---

[9] WHITE, *Christ's Object Lessons* (Washington, D.C.: RHPA, 1941), p. 69.

tutions in all lands of earth, receive the praises of men everywhere for wholesome radio and TV programs, for stop-smoking clinics, and so on. He will be satisfied as long as all this marvelous activity is not growth in grace and in that quality of life that will one day set God's people apart as His faithful witnesses and the only way to help solve the sin problem forever.

In the pages following we will study those elements in the sanctuary doctrine that make clear that God wants to do more for us than merely forgive our sins. We will see that the doctrine of righteousness by faith is indissolubly linked with the sanctuary truth and flows from it, and that experiencing the truths made clear in the sanctuary doctrine has everything to do with the hastening of the return of Jesus.

The Mediator's Twofold Role

IT IS very difficult for men and women to grasp completely or to express adequately the awesome truths implied in the fact that Jesus was "Himself the priest, Himself the victim"[1] in the plan of salvation. Paul noted His role as victim when he wrote, "He has appeared once for all at the end of the age to put away sin by the sacrifice of himself" (Hebrews 9:26). He emphasized our Lord's function as Priest when he said, "Christ has entered, not into a sanctuary made with hands, a copy of the true one, but into heaven itself, now to appear in the presence of God on our behalf" (verse 24).

As Sacrifice He provided the basis for man's salvation and made forgiveness possible; as High Priest He supplies the power to meet the conditions of salvation. Pardon and power—the "double cure."[2]

The connection between these two phases of our Lord's priesthood is exactly what Satan wants obscured:

---

[1] White, *The Desire of Ages,* p. 25.
[2] Augustus M. Toplady, "Rock of Ages," 1776. Note the ellipse of truth.

"The archdeceiver hates the great truths that bring to view an atoning sacrifice and an all-powerful mediator."[3] Misunderstanding these two vital phases has led Christians into such gross errors as widely divergent as predestination and universalism; it has misled millions by the false security of "once saved, always saved," and the "cheap grace" that inevitably follows, sooner or later, when justification is emphasized disproportionately over sanctification. Clarification occurs when we remember that justification is our title to heaven and sanctification, our fitness.

Without our Lord's death on the cross, His sacrificial atonement, there would be no salvation available for anyone (Romans 5:17–21; Acts 4:12). What He has done for all men and women could never be matched by anything that we could do, no matter how long we lived, or how earnestly we tried. But the benefits of His sacrificial atonement made for all men (1 John 2:2; 1 Timothy 2:4) apply only to those who *appropriate* His gift by faith (John 1:12; 3:16), that is, by accepting His gracious invitation to be His sons and daughters, and demonstrating their gratitude by trusting Him and obeying His will.

Our Lord's sacrificial atonement has been more generally understood by the Christian church than has His high-priestly intercession. In fact the fuller understanding of our Lord's work as Mediator (1 Timothy 2:5) has been the distinctive contribution of the Seventh-day Adventist Church, especially in view of its emphasis on the investigative, or pre-Advent, judgment as the closing phase of His intercessory work.[4]

---

[3] WHITE, *The Great Controversy*, p. 488. Note the ellipse of truth.
[4] "At-one-ment is an expression of the divine intention to destroy

The Mediator's Twofold Role

Satan is not displeased if church members emphasize the sacrificial atonement in sermons and song, if the benefits of what Christ has done *for us* are not appropriated by men and women, to be effective *"in and through us."*[5]

Therefore, we should look carefully at our Lord's intercessory, mediatorial role. His priesthood is the only link of living human relationship between God and man, the "one mediator between God and men, the man Christ Jesus" (1 Timothy 2:5). When He entered the heavenly sanctuary at His ascension, He "entered by His own blood, to shed upon His disciples the benefits of His atonement."[6]

Clearly it must be kept in mind that "the intercession of Christ in man's behalf in the sanctuary above is as essential to the plan of salvation as was His death upon the cross."[7] Why it is so essential to understand

---

sin that ruptured the universe. Restoration to oneness was not consummated at the cross. The sin problem has not yet been finally resolved. The cross is the supreme act of God for man's redemption. But that is only one aspect of Christ's work toward the final atonement. Reconciliation is effected by the living Christ. It is not something that happened two thousand years ago. At-one-ment is experienced only as men daily live a life of trust and dependence on Him. . . .

"It may be that the failure to grasp the whole work of our Lord, both on the cross and from the heavenly sanctuary, leaves man with less than a complete knowledge of all the truth the Bible reveals as to the full meaning of the atonement. . . . Both the triumph at the cross and the work of Christ as priest in heaven are the hope and pledge of final renewal and atonement."—EDWARD HEPPENSTALL, *Our High Priest,* pp. 29, 31.

[5] WHITE, *Steps to Christ,* p. 63.
[6] WHITE, *Early Writings,* p. 260.
[7] WHITE, *The Great Controversy,* p. 489. Note the ellipse of truth.

the purpose of our Lord's function as our High Priest is the purpose of this study.

His intercessory role as our High Priest is divided into two segments; the first, extending from His ascension to 1844, and the second, from 1844 to the close of probation. His work since 1844, while He continues to apply "the benefits of His mediation"[8] to those entitled to them, involves also the "last acts of His ministration in behalf of man—to perform the work of investigative judgment and to make an atonement for all who are shown to be entitled to its benefits."[9]

The questions are: What are the benefits that He has been applying since the Cross by virtue of His sacrificial atonement? and What are Christ's "last acts of His ministration" involving "the work of investigative judgment"?

As intercessory Mediator, Jesus fulfills two specific roles: (1) He silences the accusations of Satan "with arguments founded not upon our merits, but on His own"[10] His perfect life of obedience, sealed by a death that wrung the heart of God and exposed the awfulness, and the terrible end, of sin, became the basis of reconciliation and atonement between God and man. He earned the right to forgive us. (2) He is free to provide the power of grace to all those who choose to live overcoming lives. "He is the High Priest of the church, and He has a work to do which no other can perform. By His grace He is able to keep every man from transgression."[11] What more could any person ask for?

---

[8] *Ibid.,* p. 430.
[9] *Ibid.,* p. 480.
[10] WHITE, *Testimonies,* vol. 5 (Nampa, Idaho: PPPA, 1882), p. 472.
[11] WHITE, *Signs of the Times,* Feb. 14, 1900.

The Mediator's Twofold Role 47

Seen in the light of the cosmic controversy between good and evil, between the central figures, Christ and Satan, our Lord's intercessory, mediatorial work takes on great significance.[12] When Satan says that sinful men and women do not deserve forgiveness, that they are not entitled to eternal life any more than he is, that God has asked too much from His created beings and is therefore unreasonable—Jesus stands up in full view of watching worlds as the eternal answer to these questions.

What do angels and others see? They see a Man who faced Satan on his home court, who "had to be made like his brethren in every respect, so that he might become a merciful and faithful high priest" (Hebrews 2:17). They see a Man who conquered every temptation to serve Himself, proving that all men and women, with the same power available to them that He had, can live a victorious life. Our Lord's thirty-three years of perfect obedience to God's will, fighting "the battle as every child of humanity must fight it,"[13] silences every one of Satan's accusations. We have a Friend in court who has never lost a case.

In addition, Christ's powerful arm reaches out to all people who have committed the keeping of their souls to Him. He has won the right to intercede in the lives of

---

[12] "In the heavenly sanctuary all is vital, dynamic, genuine, and concerned with eternal issues. The sanctuary truth treats Satan as the real enemy, the forces of evil as real, in conflict with Christ in a war that affects every creature in the universe. Here alone the destinies of men are decided for weal or for woe. Here the realities of God's truth and purpose can be clearly seen."—HEPPENSTALL, *op. cit.*, p. 19.

[13] White, *The Desire of Ages,* p. 49.

His followers. He breaks through the power with which Satan has held them captive, developing within His faithful followers a strengthened will to resist sinful tendencies. It is the same defense by which He Himself conquered sin.

This kind of intercession men and women need now, daily, and until Jesus returns. "Everyone who will break from the slavery and service of Satan, and will stand under the blood-stained banner of Prince Immanuel will be kept by Christ's intercessions. Christ, as our Mediator, at the right hand of the Father, ever keeps us in view, for it is as necessary that He should keep us by His intercessions as that He should redeem us with His blood. If He lets go His hold of us for one moment, Satan stands ready to destroy. Those purchased by His blood, He now keeps by His intercession."[14]

Here, in the second role of the Mediator (that of

---

[14] Ellen G. White Comments, on Romans 8:34, F. D. Nichol, ed., *The Seventh-day Adventist Bible Commentary,* Vol. 6 (Washington, D.C.: RHPA, 1956), p. 1078. Of course, when the Bible or Ellen White speaks of Christ's dwelling within the Christian and providing grace to overcome sin, it should always be understood that He is doing this through His Representative, the Holy Spirit. "The Spirit was to be given as a regenerating agent, and without this the sacrifice of Christ would have been of no avail. . . . It is the Spirit that makes effectual what has been wrought out by the world's Redeemer. . . . Christ has given His Spirit as a divine power to overcome all hereditary and cultivated tendencies to evil, and to impress His own character upon His church."—WHITE, *The Desire of Ages,* p. 671. See also Ms 1, 1892, in *Manuscript Releases,* vol. 2, p. 14.

When Christ's work as Intercessor ceases at the close of probation, the Holy Spirit continues His role as the believer's Closest Friend, still providing "grace to help in time of need" (Heb. 4:16).

THE MEDIATOR'S TWOFOLD ROLE 49

providing sustaining grace to keep from sinning) rests the hope of every Christian. Through what He has done *for us,* Jesus will do His part in silencing the accusations of the accuser. But He cannot silence the accusations if we do not give Him permission to do His work *in us.*[15] John's words are simple and emphatic: "If we confess our sins, he is faithful and just to forgive us our sins, and to cleanse us from all unrighteousness" (1 John 1:9, KJV).

In commenting on this verse, Ellen White said, "The blood of Jesus Christ cleanses us from all sin. . . . We need to keep ever before us the efficacy of the blood of Jesus. That life-cleansing, life-sustaining blood, appropriated by living faith, is our hope. We need to grow in appreciation of its inestimable value, for it speaks for us only as we by faith claim its virtue, keeping the conscience clean and at peace with God."[16]

Our Lord's double role as Mediator silences Satan's charges, thus opening the door for the benefits of His life to be given to men and women, and guarantees that sufficient power is available to keep every suppliant from sin.

This double role focuses on the heart of the plan of redemption, that God's purpose is to eradicate sin from the universe.[17] This is not done by declaring it eradicated, or by sponging clean everyone's record

---

[15] "Our only ground of hope is in the righteousness of Christ imputed to us, and in that wrought by His Spirit working in and through us."—WHITE, *Steps to Christ,* p. 63.

[16] Ellen G. White Comments, on 1 John 1:7, 9, F. D. Nichol, ed., *The Seventh-day Adventist Bible Commentary,* Vol.7 (Washington, D.C.: RHPA, 1956), p. 948.

[17] The Great Controversy Theme illuminates God's plan to deal with the sin problem. When we understand how God plans to se-

with a mighty sweep of mercy. If this were so, the wisdom and justice of God Himself would be forever suspect; nothing would have been settled in the great controversy as to whether God was fair in setting up laws that no one could keep or whether He was just in irrevocably casting from heaven Satan and one third of the angels (see Revelation 12:3, 4).

The only way for sin to be destroyed while preserving both the sinner and God's justice is for the rebel to become a loyal son, willingly and habitually. Sin is a created being's clenched fist in the face of his Creator; sin is the creature distrusting God, deposing Him as the Lord of his life. The consequences of such rebellion are deadly, as the history of this dreary world reveals.

Only the sinner who confesses his sins *and* for-

---

cure the universe from any future sin problem and, thus, what the purpose of the gospel is, we no longer will be limited by the conventional theological terms that have divided the Christian world for 2,000 years.

When we grasp that "the very essence of the gospel is restoration" (ELLEN G. WHITE, in *The Desire of Ages,* p. 824) and not only forgiveness (important as that is), words such as justification and sanctification, for example, take on larger dimensions. Note how Ellen White highlights God's gospel plan: "The central theme of the Bible, the theme about which every other in the whole book clusters, is the redemption plan, [that is,] the restoration in the human soul of the image of God. From the first intimation of hope in the sentence pronounced in Eden to that last glorious promise in the Revelation, 'They shall see His face; and His name shall be in their foreheads,' the burden of every book and every passage of the Bible is the unfolding of this wondrous theme,—man's uplifting,—'which giveth us the victory through our Lord Jesus Christ.' He who grasps this thought has before him an infinite field of study. He has the key that will unlock to him the whole treasure-house of God's word."—*Education* (Nampa, Idaho: PPPA, 1942), pp. 125, 126. See also p. 190.

The Mediator's Twofold Role

sakes them "shall have mercy" (Proverbs 28:13, KJV). God is not interested in destroying men and women; His first goal is to save them, to rescue them from their self-centeredness, to appeal to their better judgment, and to restore them to a happy, willing relationship of trust.

But one thing that God cannot overlook is sham. Nothing is settled if church members claim the name of Christ, but not His power; or claim His power, but not His character.[18]

For this reason Ellen White emphasized a fundamental biblical doctrine when she wrote, "The religion of Christ means more than the forgiveness of sin; it means taking away our sins, and filling the vacuum with the graces of the Holy Spirit."[19]

The intercessory work of Jesus as our "all-powerful mediator" not only applies to supplicating sinners the forgiveness made possible by His atoning sacrifice, it also supplies the power through the Holy Spirit by which those sins are truly eradicated from the character of trusting, willing Christians.[20] This astounding thought can never be repeated enough; yet it is rarely heard

---

[18] "Lucifer desired God's power, but not His character."—WHITE, *The Desire of Ages,* p. 435.

[19] WHITE, *Christ's Object Lessons,* pp. 419, 420. "To be pardoned in the way that Christ pardons, is not only to be forgiven, but to be renewed in the spirit of our mind."—WHITE, *Review and Herald,* August 19, 1890.

"The grace of Christ purifies while it pardons, and fits men for a holy heaven."—WHITE, *That I May Know Him* (Washington, D.C.: RHPA, 1964), p. 336.

[20] "Through the perfect obedience of the Son of God, through the merits of His blood, and the power of His intercession, man may become a partaker of the divine nature."—WHITE, *Signs of the Times,* July 6, 1888.

throughout the pages of church history. It is the truth that Satan fears most.[21]

No wonder Satan is delighted when the sanctuary truths are mystified, obscured, or set aside as a boring subject. No wonder Ellen White wrote, "All need to become more intelligent in regard to the work of the atonement, which is going on in the sanctuary above. When this grand truth is seen and understood, those who hold it will work in harmony with Christ to prepare a people to stand in the great day of God, and their efforts will be successful."[22]

This work of preparing "a people to stand in the great day of God" can be best understood in terms of the sanctuary doctrine. The task of making this clear to the world has been assigned to Seventh-day Adventists.

The following chapters will examine this more specifically.

---

[21] Ellen White focused on these great issues that Satan wants obscured: "If those who hide and excuse their faults could see how Satan exults over them, how he taunts Christ and holy angels with their course, they would make haste to confess their sins and to put them away. Through defects in the character, Satan works to gain control of the whole mind, and he knows that if these defects are cherished, he will succeed. Therefore he is constantly seeking to deceive the followers of Christ with his fatal sophistry that it is impossible for them to overcome. But Jesus pleads in their behalf His wounded hands, His bruised body; and He declares to all who would follow Him, 'My grace is sufficient for thee.' 'Take My yoke upon you and learn of Me; for I am meek and lowly in heart: and ye shall find rest unto your souls. For My yoke is easy, and My burden is light.' Let none, then, regard their defects as incurable. God will give faith and grace to overcome them."—*The Great Controversy,* p. 489.

[22] *Testimonies,* vol. 5, p. 575.

God's Purpose Through a Symbol

TO BETTER understand the larger purpose of the Christian church in general, and the Seventh-day Adventist movement in particular, as well as the grand goal of the plan of salvation, we should reflect further upon why God gave the earthly sanctuary to the Israelites in Old Testament times.

The earthly sanctuary service symbolized, in almost sandbox, kindergarten clarity, how God planned to deal with the sin problem as it relates to individuals, the earth, Satan, and the whole universe. God's foremost concern is that His reasoning creation will one day be free from the chains and anxieties of sin, and purged from all doubt regarding His love and wisdom. But He knows that this will come about, not by decree, but by the free choice of those who are settled into the truth about Him and who act accordingly.

How could God get His solution to the sin problem across to rebel, earth-oriented men and women? Write it on the clouds? Thunder it daily across the Sinai wilderness at dawn? No. Knowing how we learn and retain knowledge most effectively, He did what was best, even though less spectacular and overwhelming than thunder or cloud-writing. He gave us a picture story wrapped up in human drama, an object lesson that could be seen, heard, experienced, and referred to over and over again, in case the memory was weak or the learning powers slow.

After revealing to Israel His program of life, liberty, and happiness in the Ten Commandments, backgrounded by the thunder and lightning of Sinai, He knew that the law would only overwhelm sinners. He knew that its expectations would only increase man's sense of helplessness and despair. So immediately He ordered the building of the earthly tabernacle to teach the twofold lesson that we have been discussing in this book—"the lesson of pardon of sin, and power through the Saviour for obedience unto life."[1] Pardon and power, the twofold role and gifts of our all-powerful Mediator, were just what the Israelites needed—and what we need today!

In this awesome sanctuary service "God desired His people to read His purpose for the human soul. It was the same purpose long afterward set forth by the apostle Paul, speaking by the Holy Spirit: 'Know ye not that ye are the temple of God, and that the Spirit of God dwelleth in you? If any man defile the temple of God, him shall God destroy; for the temple of God is holy, which temple ye are.' "[2]

The Jerusalem Temple in Christ's day was intended to continue serving the same function as the earthly sanctuary: "That temple, erected for the abode of the divine Presence, was designed to be an object lesson for Israel and for the world. From eternal ages it was God's

---

[1] WHITE, *Education,* p. 36. Note the ellipse of truth.
[2] *Ibid.*

God's Purpose Through a Symbol

purpose that every created being, from the bright and holy seraph to man, should be a temple for the indwelling of the Creator. Because of sin, humanity ceased to be a temple for God. . . . But by the incarnation of the Son of God, the purpose of Heaven is fulfilled. God dwells in humanity, and through saving grace the heart of man becomes again His temple. God designed that the temple at Jerusalem should be a continual witness to the high destiny open to every soul. . . . In cleansing the temple from the world's buyers and sellers, Jesus announced His mission to cleanse the heart from the defilement of sin—from the earthly desires, the selfish lusts, the evil habits, that corrupt the soul. . . . No man can of himself cast out the evil throng that have taken possession of the heart. Only Christ can cleanse the soul temple. But He will not force an entrance. He comes not into the heart as to the temple of old; but He says, 'Behold, I stand at the door, and knock: if any man hear My voice, and open the door, I will come in to him.' Rev. 3:20."[3]

One of the purposes for our Lord's incarnation was to give us an additional object lesson, this time in flesh and blood: to demonstrate (1) how God wanted to relate to men and women, and (2) what God expected from men and women. In so doing, He fulfilled the purpose of which the tabernacle was a symbol.[4]

---

[3] WHITE, *The Desire of Ages,* p. 161.

[4] *Ibid.* "By coming to dwell with us, Jesus was to reveal God both to men and to angels. He was the Word of God,—God's thought made audible . . . So Christ set up His tabernacle in the midst of our human encampment. He pitched His tent by the side of the tents of men, that He might dwell among us, and make us familiar with His divine character and life."—*Ibid.,* pp. 19-23.

What the sanctuary service taught in symbols, Jesus exemplified. What Jesus exemplified, His followers are to reflect.[5]

In every respect, by His life and death, Jesus met the demands of justice and made it possible for God to be "just and the justifier of the one who has faith in Jesus" (Romans 3:26, NASB).[6] He exposed Satan's lies

---

[5] "As one of us He was to give an example of obedience. For this He took upon Himself our nature, and passed through our experiences. 'In all things it behooved Him to be made like unto His brethren.' Heb. 2:17. If we had to bear anything which Jesus did not endure, then upon this point Satan would represent the power of God as insufficient for us. Therefore Jesus was 'in all points tempted like as we are.' Heb. 4:15. He endured every trial to which we are subject. And He exercised in His own behalf no power that is not freely offered to us. As man, He met temptation, and overcame in the strength given Him from God. He says, 'I delight to do thy will, O My God: yea, thy law is within My heart.' Ps. 40:8. As He went about doing good, and healing all who were afflicted by Satan, He made plain to men the character of God's law and the nature of His service. His life testifies that it is possible for us also to obey the law of God.

"By His humanity, Christ touched humanity; by His divinity, He lays hold upon the throne of God. As the Son of man, He gave us an example of obedience; as the Son of God, He gives us power to obey."—*Ibid.*, p. 24.

[6] Our Lord's sinless life lived under all the conditions common to fallen men and women must never be separated from the attention we give to His death. His death would have been relatively insignificant without His perfect obedience as a truly human being. His death for us, enough to drain out of any honest man or woman the last drops of their gratitude, is the focal point of the plan of redemption because it was the truly human, perfectly obedient, Jesus who died. "Satan, claiming the world as his rightful territory, sought by every device to wrench it from the Redeemer's grasp; but by His life and death of humiliation Christ held it fast."—WHITE, *Signs of the Times*, Feb. 14, 1900.

"Through Jesus, God's mercy was manifested to men; but mercy does not set aside justice. The law reveals the attributes of God's

God's Purpose Through a Symbol 57

by demonstrating that God was not expecting the impossible when He asked for obedience from His creation; the life of Jesus proved that human beings can live an obedient, overcoming life.[7]

---

character, and not a jot or tittle of it could be changed to meet man in his fallen condition. . . .

"The law requires righteousness,—a righteous life, a perfect character; and this man has not to give. He cannot meet the claims of God's holy law. But Christ, coming to the earth as man, lived a holy life, and developed a perfect character. These He offers as a free gift to all who will receive them. His life stands for the life of man. Thus they have remission of sins that are past, through the forbearance of God. . . . By His life and His death, Christ proved that God's justice did not destroy His mercy, but that sin could be forgiven, and that the law is righteous, and can be perfectly obeyed."—WHITE, *The Desire of Ages,* p. 762.

"By His spotless life, His obedience, His death on the cross of Calvary, Christ interceded for the lost race."—WHITE, *Christ's Object Lessons,* p. 156.

"He [the Father] is satisfied with the atonement made. He is glorified by the incarnation, the life, death, and mediation of His Son."—WHITE, *Testimonies,* vol. 6, p. 364.

[7] "Satan had claimed that it was impossible for man to obey God's commandments; and in our own strength it is true that we cannot obey them. But Christ came in the form of humanity, and by His perfect obedience He proved that humanity and divinity combined can obey every one of God's precepts."—WHITE, *Christ's Object Lessons,* p. 314.

"After the fall of man, Satan declared that human beings were proved to be incapable of keeping the law of God, and he sought to carry the universe with him in this belief. Satan's words appeared to be true, and Christ came to unmask the deceiver. The Majesty of heaven undertook the cause of man, and with the same facilities that man may obtain, withstood the temptations of Satan as man must withstand them. This was the only way in which fallen man could become a partaker of the divine nature. In taking human nature, Christ was fitted to understand man's trials and sorrows and all the temptations wherewith he is beset. . . . He felt the strength of this temptation; He met it in our behalf, and con-

What Jesus has done *for* us in terms of His sacrificial life and death is revealed in the services of the wilderness tabernacle and the subsequent temples in Jerusalem. These lessons we can but contemplate with awe and receive with gratitude. What He has wanted to do *in* us awaits only our cooperation in permitting Him to accomplish His work in cleansing the soul temple.

These dual aspects of our Lord's role as Redeemer are even more clearly defined when we study how the earthly sanctuary service also symbolized the Christian church.

At the turn of the century Ellen White outlined an interesting connection between the earthly sanctuary service and the Christian church. In part she wrote: "The Jewish tabernacle was a type of the Christian church. . . . The church on earth, composed of those who are faithful and loyal to God, is the 'true tabernacle,' whereof the Redeemer is the minister. God, and not man, pitched this tabernacle on a high, elevated platform. This tabernacle is Christ's body, and from north, south, east, and west, He gathers those who shall help to compose it.

"Through Christ the true believers are represented as being built together for an habitation of God through the Spirit. Paul writes: [Eph. 2:4-22 is quoted]. . . .

"Altho[ugh] the plan of salvation was carried for-

---

quered. And He used only the weapons justifiable for human beings to use—the word of Him who is mighty in counsel—'It is written.' . . . Christ's humanity would demonstrate for eternal ages the question which settled the controversy."—WHITE, *Selected Messages,* book 1, pp. 251-255.

ward according to the plan ordained from the foundation of the earth, yet men and women will not be saved unless they themselves exercise faith, and build on the true foundation, unless they allow God to re-create them by His Holy Spirit. God works in and through the human agent who cooperates with Him by choosing to help to compose the Lord's building. A holy tabernacle is built up of those who receive Christ as their personal Saviour. . . . By receiving Christ and being conformed to His will, man goes on to perfection. This building up of individual characters, which are renewed, constitutes a structure more noble than any mortal workmanship. Thus the great work of God goes forward from point to point. Those who desire a place in His church show this by their willingness to be so conformed to His will that they can be trusted with grace to impart to others. . . .

"Christ is the Minister of the true tabernacle, the High Priest of all who believe in Him as a personal Saviour; and His office no other can take. He is the High Priest of the church, and He has a work to do which no other can perform. By His grace He is able to keep every man from transgression. His ambassadors, those who receive Him, are born again, and are thus fitted to represent Him [Heb. 7:26-28]."[8]

These words highlight some very important aspects of the plan of salvation, especially as seen through the symbolism of the sanctuary service. Without diminishing whatsoever the fact that Jesus is the Minister of the " 'true tabernacle' in heaven, to which the earthly sanc-

---

[8] "God's Care for His Church." *Signs of the Times,* Feb. 14, 1900.

tuary pointed," or that "the 'true tabernacle' in heaven is the sanctuary of the new covenant,"[9] Ellen White here makes another application of His role as the Minister of the true tabernacle. The "true tabernacle" in this application is the church on earth, composed of persons who are permitting His grace to keep them from transgression, truly born again people who are thus being fitted to represent Him.

From the inauguration of the wilderness tabernacle to the Jerusalem temples, God's followers knew that the plan of salvation symbolized in the sanctuary service concerned people, not animals, drapery, wood, or water. The literal aspects of the sanctuary doctrine taught very literal truths about how God deals with men and women. He doesn't clean and restore furniture, but people. The glorious truths symbolized in the earthly sanctuary refer to very literal acts, events, and relationships that exist between God and His people.[10]

While Jesus is in a very real place in heaven, performing very real functions in the outworking of the great controversy, one of His chief concerns relating to the climax of the great controversy is the building up of His church on earth. The earthly sanctuary was a shadow (Hebrews 8:5) of these great truths seen in

---

[9] *The Great Controversy,* p. 417.
[10] "The heavenly temple, the abiding place of the King of kings, where 'thousand thousands ministered unto Him, and ten thousand times ten thousand stood before Him,' (Daniel 7:10), that temple filled with the glory of the eternal throne, where seraphim, its shining guardians, veil their faces in adoration—no earthly structure could represent its vastness and its glory. Yet important truths concerning the heavenly sanctuary and the great work there carried forward for man's redemption were to be taught by the earthly sanctuary and its services."—WHITE, *Patriarchs and Prophets* (Nampa, Idaho: PPPA, 1913), p. 357.

the noonday sun of the New Testament and further clarified in the writings of Ellen White. To see these truths in their clearest light, we need not unduly dwell on the details of the earthly sanctuary; we should go to those later revelations that interpret and clarify the shadow.

Ellen White and others have pointed out that God is primarily concerned with people; that all His teaching devices represent both His part and man's role in the great controversy.[11] The object of salvation is to have a cleansed, redeemed people. The purpose of the sanctuary service and doctrine was to clarify

---

[11] Arthur Spalding, author of *Origin and History of Seventh-day Adventists,* wrote: "We cannot, of course, suppose that the heavenly sanctuary is like the structure of the earthly sanctuary. It is infinitely more glorious, supernal, beyond the grasp of man's mind. . . .

"There was the type, the shadow of the real; what we call the antitype is the reality. The sanctuary as a whole represents the relationship of God to man in the work of redemption. The service in the first apartment, the holy place, is the mediation of Christ for His people in all generations; the service on the Day of Atonement in the second apartment, the most holy place, is the concluding work of Christ's ministry in preparation for the final abolition of sin at the executive judgment. . . .

"We speak of all this in the language of men; for only so, by symbol and speech, could God convey any idea to men of the great work of the atonement and the judgment. Human mind cannot grasp the realities of that heavenly scene of judgment: the books of God—not like our books or records, but inerrant and complete; the symbolic blood—not actual blood but the life which the blood signifies; the holy place and the most holy—not rooms as we conceive them but the ineffable abode of the great God and His ministering spirits; the day of atonement—not a literal day, but a period the length of which is known only to God. And so, with all the other symbols and ceremonies."—Volume 1 (Washington, D.C.: RHPA, 1961), pp. 108-111.

Heppenstall commented: "The nature and meaning of the heav-

this marvelous goal and to provide a clear explanation as to how sincere men and women could reach that goal.

God is concerned with the eradication of sin from the universe. The living proof that sin is unnecessary, that men and women can overcome all tendencies to sin, that God has been fair in expecting obedience as the test of faith, has been demonstrated in the life of Jesus. It will be doubly vouched for in the lives of His followers, especially during that generation that hears the pronouncement "He that is righteous, let him be righteous still" (Revelation 22:11, KJV) just before the close of probation.

In the 1900 *Signs* article previously quoted, Ellen White merely re-emphasized a towering principle that she often expressed—that the Israelites (and Christians ever since) were to read God's "purpose for the human soul,"[12] in the building of the desert sanctuary or in an awesome temple in Jerusalem. That same purpose, Mrs. White said, was set forth by Paul when he wrote, "Know ye not that ye are the temple of God, and that the Spirit of God dwelleth in you?" (1 Corinthians 3:16, KJV).

Just as God's people were to cooperate with Him

---

enly sanctuary cannot be established by scientific data. No amount of detailed knowledge of the materials and measurements of the earthly sanctuary can adequately represent heavenly things or reproduce God's work upon His throne. We see in the earthly sanctuary no full and decisive revelation of our great High Priest in heaven. Christ is not engaged in lighting lamps, turning over loaves of bread, or swinging incense burners. The realities do not reside in places, materials, or architectural design, but in the divine activity brought to bear upon the living situations of the great controversy itself."—*Our High Priest,* p. 20.

[12] WHITE, *Education,* p. 36.

God's Purpose Through a Symbol

and with one another in the building of the earthly sanctuaries, so they must cooperate with Him in the development of "God's temple in the soul."[13] Just as God dwelt in the earthly sanctuaries, so He desires to make the human soul a fit place for the habitation of the Spirit of God.

This divine-human cooperation is the only way salvation first comes to men and women through justification and the only way it is maintained in sanctification. "God works in and through the human agent who cooperates with Him by choosing to help to compose the Lord's building. A holy tabernacle is built up of those who receive Christ as their personal Saviour."[14]

But is this building-up process an overweening concentration on the individual, a polishing of the piety of church members while multitudes die unwarned? Not so! Not for a moment! Those who are concerned about fulfilling God's purpose for them, concerned about how best to cooperate with God in re-creating their character after the Pattern, are the persons God can truly work in and through for the completion of the gospel commission.[15] As Mrs. White wrote in her 1900 *Signs* article: "Those who desire a place in His church show this by their willingness to be so conformed to His will that they can be trusted with grace to impart to others."

God is in the process of preparing human instruments who want His character, as well as His power.

---

[13] *Ibid.,* p. 37.
[14] WHITE, *Signs of the Times,* Feb. 14, 1900.
[15] "Our only ground of hope is in the righteousness of Christ imputed to us, and in that wrought by His Spirit working in and through us."—WHITE, *Steps to Christ,* p. 63.

When they have developed such characters He will be able to trust them as His exhibits of grace (Ephesians 1:4-14). For only then will His people reveal, undeniably and beyond question, the truth about what He can do for lost sinners.[16]

The successful completion of the gospel commission as promised in Matthew 24:14 largely depends on Christians with whom God will not be embarrassed to identify in the day of His power. Becoming men and women God can trust with His power not only will prepare them for fitness to live in His kingdom but also will set the stage for God to give Planet Earth its last warning message. Mature Christians are Christlike. They are the overcomers who respond to the Laodicean message (Revelation 3:14-21)—the only ones on earth who are consistently moved, and spontaneously constrained, to proclaim the gospel in its fullness to their fellow men.

The urgency resting upon Adventists because of these truths will be discussed in the next chapter.

---

[16] Often, in words similar to these, the Adventist Church has been challenged: "By revealing in our own life the character of Christ we cooperate with Him in the work of saving souls. It is only by revealing in our life His character that we can cooperate with Him. . . . When those who profess to serve God follow Christ's example, practicing the principles of the law in their daily life; when every act bears witness that they love God supremely and their neighbor as themselves, then will the church have power to move the world."—WHITE, *Christ's Object Lessons,* p. 340.

The Vindication of God

EVERY thoughtful Christian knows that Jesus, in His life and death, vindicated the character and judgment of God. His "death proved God's administration and government to be without a flaw. Satan's charge in regard to the conflicting attributes of justice and mercy was forever settled beyond question."[1]

Satan's charges had included "that God was unjust, that His law was faulty, and that the good of the universe required it to be changed." The purpose of the plan of salvation involved more "than the salvation of man." Christ came to earth, not only to validate the fairness of God's law for humanity, but to "vindicate the character of God before the universe" and thus "justify God and His Son in their dealing with the rebellion of Satan."[2]

But when Christ died, the controversy was not yet over. Even though Jesus, having taken "the results of

---

[1] WHITE, *Signs of the Times,* July 12, 1899.
[2] WHITE, *Patriarchs and Prophets,* pp. 69, 70. See WHITE, *Steps to Christ,* pp. 10, 11.

the working of the great law of heredity," had proved that God's law was fair and could be obeyed by the sons and daughters of Adam,[3] the controversy was not then over. If it were over, why would God let time go on with all the human suffering and horror of the past 2,000 years? Why would even God want to endure His own incredible suffering in watching this unspeakable horror, if Jesus had settled all the questions in the great controversy?

Although the Cross broke the "last link of sympathy between Satan and the heavenly world," Satan was "not then destroyed." Why? Because "the angels did not even then understand all that was involved in the great controversy." What more was needed? "The principles at stake were to be more fully revealed."[4]

In other words, God was looking down to Judgment Day. On that Day all created beings, all angels good and bad, all the inhabitants of unfallen worlds and earth, will take one long, final look at how God "vindicated" His character in the face of Satan's deceptive charges.

God knew that Satan would charge that Jesus did not really prove anything because he conceded that *Jesus had only proven what God could do* under human conditions, not what created beings could do without the advantage of divine lineage.

God knew that such questions had to be settled forever. He also knew that He had to prove that even sinful human beings could find courage in the words and example of Jesus and could, by the same Spirit that kept Jesus from sinning, keep them from sinning. Such a

---

[3] WHITE, *The Desire of Ages,* pp. 49, 24.
[4] *Ibid.,* p. 761.

THE VINDICATION OF GOD 67

record of faithfulness would settle all questions forever regarding His fairness, mercy, and "grace to help in time of need" (Heb. 4:16).[5]

God also knew that before He could bring history to a close, He would have to have His message about His goodness and fairness proclaimed clearly throughout the world. Why? Because He would not want anyone in those last days before He ended history to raise the question: "How come I am declared lost when I never had a chance to know what I was rejecting? If I had had more time to live, I might have had a better chance to grow up but you came before I had a fair chance to respond to your invitations. In other words, God, You never gave me a fair chance to say Yes or No like those commandment keepers You are saving had!"

The intent of this chapter is to take a quick look at what is involved in the final settling of the great controversy before Jesus returns—because God will surely not return if something is still not settled! That is why, since 1844, a special urgency has rested upon those who perceive that God waits for a generation of people who

---

[5] In 1894, Ellen White noted how Christ needed His church to help Him "bruise the head of the serpent": "Christ was the special One who should bruise the head of the serpent; but the prophecy also includes all those who shall overcome the enemy by the blood of the Lamb, and by the word of their testimony. . . . Those who truly unite with Christ will be found doing the same work that Christ did while on earth,—they will be found magnifying the law and making it honorable. But those who stand to vindicate the honor of God's law will be objects of Satan's enmity. . . . Whenever a soul takes a decided stand for truth, the head of the serpent is bruised by the seed of the woman. . . . When the advocates of truth reveal the efficiency of truth in their life and character, a blow is struck against the kingdom of Satan."—*The Youth's Instructor,* October 11, 1894.

seriously respond to the heavenly call to delay the Advent in Revelation 7 "till we have sealed the servants of our God on their foreheads" (Rev. 7:3). These people who help settle the great controversy and vindicate the character of God are called, "those who keep the commandments of God and the faith of Jesus" (Rev. 14:12). Many are the counsels[6] to the church that emphasize the direct relationship between Christ's work in the Most Holy Place and His work in the lives of His followers on earth:

"Now Christ is in the heavenly sanctuary. And what is He doing? Making atonement for us, cleansing the sanctuary from the sins of the people. Then we must enter by faith into the sanctuary with Him, we must commence the work in the sanctuary of our souls. We are to cleanse ourselves from all defilement. We must 'cleanse ourselves from all filthiness of the flesh and spirit, perfecting holiness in the fear of God.' "[7]

One of the most urgent messages of the sanctuary doctrine to Christians since 1844 is that some-

---

[6] "This is the great day of atonement, and our Advocate is standing before the Father, pleading as our intercessor. In place of wrapping about us the garments of self-righteousness, we should be found daily humbling ourselves before God, confessing our own individual sins, seeking the pardon of our transgressions, and cooperating with Christ in the work of preparing our souls to reflect the divine image. Unless we enter the sanctuary above, and unite with Christ in working out our own salvation with fear and trembling, we shall be weighed in the balances of the sanctuary, and shall be pronounced wanting."—ELLEN G. WHITE Comments, on Hebrews 10:19–21, F. D. Nichol, ed., *The Seventh-day Adventist Bible Commentary,* Vol. 7, pp. 933, 934.

[7] WHITE, sermon delivered October 20, 1888. Reprinted in A. V. Olson, *Through Crisis to Victory* (Washington, D.C.: RHPA, 1966), p. 267.

thing special is required of God's followers in terms of character development that may not have been so crucial to the development of the church heretofore. God's people attaining the quality of faithfulness that He waits for, and for which He will give them every needed divine power to achieve, significantly affects how soon Jesus can finish His work in the Most Holy Place.[8]

The urgency that should be gripping God's people on earth rests on the solemn fact that, in entering the Most Holy Place in 1844, our High Priest began the last phase of His mediatorial work which involves the character fitness of the last generation. It was God's plan to complete this work many years ago. The delay has not been due to heavenly inefficiency or a change in His plans.[9] He longs to pour out the latter rain on those who have cleansed "the soul temple of

---

[8] This point regarding the relationship of character development and the hastening or delaying of the Second Advent will be discussed in the chapter entitled, "Why Time Lingers."

[9] "Had Adventists, after the great disappointment in 1844, held fast their faith and followed on unitedly in the opening providence of God, receiving the message of the third angel and in the power of the Holy Spirit proclaiming it to the world, they would have seen the salvation of God, the Lord would have wrought mightily with their efforts, the work would have been completed, and Christ would have come ere this to receive His people to their reward. But in the period of doubt and uncertainty that followed the disappointment, many of the advent believers yielded their faith. . . . Thus the work was hindered, and the world was left in darkness. Had the whole Adventist body united upon the commandments of God and the faith of Jesus, how widely different would have been our history!

"It was not the will of God that the coming of Christ should be thus delayed. God did not design that His people, Israel, should wander forty years in the wilderness. He promised to lead them

every defilement."[10] He longs for His people to be so settled into the truth,[11] so comfortable with His way of life, that He can impart His seal of approval and point to them without embarrassment in a worldwide mission appeal, "Here are they that keep the commandments of God, and the faith of Jesus" (Revelation 14:12, KJV). He longs to announce the end of the great controversy: "He that is unjust, let him be unjust still: and he which is filthy, let him be filthy still: and he that is righteous, let him be righteous still: and he that is holy, let him by holy still" (chapter 22:11, KJV).

---

directly to the land of Canaan, and establish them there a holy, healthy, happy people. But those to whom it was first preached, went not in 'because of unbelief.' Their hearts were filled with murmuring, rebellion, and hatred, and He could not fulfill His covenant with them. . . .

"The same sins have delayed the entrance of moden Israel into the heavenly Canaan. In neither case were the promises of God at fault. It is the unbelief, the worldliness, unconsecration, and strife among the Lord's professed people that have kept us in this world of sin and sorrow so many years."—WHITE, *Evangelism,* pp. 695, 696.

"It is the privilege of every Christian, not only to look for, but to hasten the coming of our Lord Jesus Christ. Were all who profess His name bearing fruit to His glory, how quickly the whole world would be sown with the seed of the gospel. Quickly the last harvest would be ripened, and Christ would come to gather the precious grain."—WHITE, *Testimonies,* vol. 8, p. 22.

[10] WHITE, *Ibid.,* vol. 5, p. 214.

[11] "Just as soon as the people of God are sealed in their foreheads—it is not any seal or mark that can be seen, but a settling into the truth, both intellectually and spiritually, so they cannot be moved—just as soon as God's people are sealed and prepared for the shaking, it will come."—Ellen G. White Comments, on Ezekiel 9:2-4, F. D. Nichol, ed., *The Seventh-day Adventist Bible Commentary,* Vol. 4, p. 1161.

The Vindication of God

Since 1844 Jesus has been waiting for a people over whose individual records in the heavenly sanctuary He can write "Cleansed"; a people who would reflect His concern for the salvation and well-being of others, through whom all heaven could freely work without embarrassing the Father's name, in completing the gospel commission.[12]

Every day the life pattern of the professed Christian is being reflected on those records in the Most Holy Place. The urgent question arises: Is it a record that reflects a person who, by the grace of God, is overcoming sin or not? "Through the grace of God and their own diligent effort they must be conquerors in the battle with evil. While the investigative judgment is going forward in heaven, while the sins of penitent believers are being removed from the sanctuary, there is to be a special work of purification, of putting away of sin, among God's people upon earth. . . . When this work shall have been accomplished, the followers of Christ will be ready for His appearing."[13]

In general, the sanctuary service has been God's teaching device, instructing us that He will pardon our transgressions and empower us to live a life of

---

[12] "Christ is waiting with longing desire for the manifestation of Himself in His church. When the character of Christ shall be perfectly reproduced in His people, then He will come to claim them as His own. It is the privilege of every Christian not only to look for but to hasten the coming of our Lord Jesus Christ. Were all who profess His name bearing fruit to His glory, how quickly the whole world would be sown with the seed of the gospel. Quickly the last great harvest would be ripened, and Christ would come to gather the precious grain."—WHITE, *Christ's Object Lessons,* p. 69.

[13] WHITE, *The Great Controversy,* p. 425.

Christlike obedience.[14] He will do the cleansing, the empowering, the keeping from sin, if we choose to let Him work. The cleansed overcomer will reflect both the character of Jesus and His unstinting life of service.

Specifically, the work of Jesus as our High Priest in the Most Holy Place, has a direct relationship with that movement on earth that is not only announcing the judgment hour message of Revelation 14:6-14 but also permitting the grace of God to do His glorious work in overcoming sin.

Could any time be more glorious, more exciting, more personally satisfying, than now?[15]

Basic to Adventist thought for more than a century have been these twin concepts of a cleansed sanc-

---

[14] "Another lesson the tabernacle, through its service of sacrifice, was to teach—the lesson of pardon of sin, and power through the Saviour for obedience unto life."—WHITE, *Education,* p. 36.

[15] "The scenes connected with the sanctuary above should make such an impression upon the minds and hearts of all that they may be able to impress others. All need to become more intelligent in regard to the work of the atonement, which is going on in the sanctuary above. When this grand truth is seen and understood, those who hold it will work in harmony with Christ to prepare a people to stand in the great day of God, and their efforts will be successful. By study, contemplation, and prayer God's people will be elevated above common, earthly thoughts and feelings, and will be brought into harmony with Christ and His great work of cleansing the sanctuary above from the sins of the people. Their faith will go with Him into the sanctuary, and the worshipers on earth will be carefully reviewing their lives and comparing their characters with the great standard of righteousness. They will see their own defects; they will also see that they must have the aid of the Spirit of God if they would become qualified for the great and solemn work for this time which is laid upon God's ambassadors."—WHITE, *Testimonies,* vol. 5, p. 575.

tuary and a prepared people. With these concepts Adventist scholars have closely connected such ideas as "the blotting out of sins," "the refreshing," and "the wedding garment which is the righteousness of the saints."

Early in Adventist history Joseph Bates expounded on the connection between the sanctuary type and antitype, especially regarding the cleansing of the sanctuary on the Day of Atonement. After quoting Leviticus 16:16 he wrote: "Will the reader please read these eighteen words again, and see if he cannot tell the meaning of the *cleansing of the Sanctuary*. Oh yes! You say, it was to cleanse the people, all of them, from their sins. Very well, do not forget it, when it comes down to you in the antitype."[16]

Stephen N. Haskell, in 1856, also saw clearly the connection between a prepared people and the completion of the gospel commission: "A theory of the Third Angel's Message never, no never, will save us, without the wedding garment, which is the righteousness of the saints. We must perfect holiness in the fear of the Lord."[17]

At the 1901 General Conference, Haskell gave a series of studies on the history of the sanctuary doctrine. During his summation of basic Adventist thought on this subject he said, "We have learned first that there is a time that Christ will enter the heavenly temple; second, that that time will be the investigative judg-

---

[16] "Midnight Cry in the Past," *Review and Herald,* December, 1850, p. 21. In this same article Bates pointed out that the "cleansing" of God's people would take place before the seven last plagues.

[17] "A Few Thoughts on the Philadelphia and Laodicean Churches," *Review and Herald,* Nov. 6, 1856, p. 6.

ment; third, that the work during that period will be the perfection of character; and fourth, the more you can understand about that temple work, the more you will understand the power of the truth of God that relates to God's people and to this time in which we live."[18]

In 1864, a remarkable series of articles appeared in the *Review,* authored by D. T. Bourdeau, in which he emphasized the special responsibilities resting on the last generation church: "Some do not see the necessity of receiving the truths applicable to the present time in order to be sanctified. They think

---

[18] "Bible Study," *General Conference Bulletin,* April 7, 1901, p. 100. Later in 1901, in a series of *Review* articles, Haskell emphasized the same theme, that a prepared people on earth corresponds to a cleansed sanctuary in heaven: "The knowledge which they [the Jews] lacked was the spiritual application of the sanctuary question, which centered in Christ. The sanctuary question was to reveal Christ, His work in the heavenly courts, and as it would be carried on in the hearts of His disciples. It is thus apparent that the work in the hearts of the people must correspond with that of Christ in heaven.

"There are three temples brought to view in the Bible, and all should be blended into one study . . . The work of Christ in heaven is also to go forward in the living temple of His people on the earth; so while there was a sanctuary on the earth, and still one in heaven, the most important of the three is His people; for the object of the earthly sanctuary was to teach man how to know and believe the actual work done for him in the heavenly sanctuary. . . All the work revealed by the typical temple shadowing the real work of Christ in heaven is for the purification of His Church on the earth, and consequently a neglect of a knowledge of these truths will leave men unprepared for the impending judgments of God, as really as the Jews were unprepared for the destruction that came upon them."—"The Sanctuary Question from the Standpoint of the Book of Hebrews," *Review and Herald,* Aug. 13, 1901.

THE VINDICATION OF GOD

they can be sanctified by living as other good Christians have lived. But how have good Christians in the past been sanctified? Have they not been sanctified by living up to the light that they had in their day? And if we are favored with more light than they were, if God has other duties for us to perform, can we be sanctified by merely living as they lived? Does God cause light to shine on His word in vain? . . . It will require a special preparation to meet the Lord when He comes."[19]

Although we have referred to only a few of the early Adventist thinkers on the subject of the sanctuary, many more could be cited. Their general understanding had a remarkable unity and fullness. They saw early and expounded forcefully that the cleansing of the sanctuary in heaven was directly related to the development of a cleansed, prepared people on earth. They argued convincingly that God was waiting for a people who would faithfully reflect the goodness of those who kept His commandments and who met all the problems and temptations of life with the same faith that Jesus had.[20] The latter-rain refreshing would be experienced only after, and as a result of, this character preparation. Such prepara-

---

[19] "Sanctification: or Living Holiness," *Review and Herald,* Aug. 2, 1864.

[20] Early Adventist thinkers were not dispensationalists. They did not teach that God had a higher standard for this last generation of commandment keepers. But they did teach the difference between preparing people to die and preparing people to be translated. What overcomers of all ages have experienced, such as Enoch, Elijah, and Job, will be mirrored during this last generation by a significant number of people who create a critical mass through whom the Spirit can work—such a period is called "the time of the latter rain," or "the loud cry."

tion would be a divinely assisted attainment reflected in the heavenly sanctuary by the "blotting out" of those sins that once plagued the lives of the overcomers.

W. W. Prescott was especially clear in his understanding of the connection between the third angel's message of Revelation 14, the blotting out of sins, an overcoming people, and the time when the Lord will return. In a sermon at the 1903 General Conference he said: "There is a difference between the gospel being preached for the forgiveness of sins and the gospel being preached for the blotting out of sin. Always, and today, there is abundant provision for the forgiveness of sins. In our generation comes the provision for the blotting out of sin. And the blotting out of sin is what will prepare the way for the coming of the Lord; and the blotting out of sin is the ministry of our high Priest in the Most Holy Place in the heavenly sanctuary; and it makes a difference to the people of God today in their ministry, in their message, and in their experience, whether they recognize the change of the ministry from one apartment to the other, or whether they recognize and experience the fact of the change. . . .

"Now that should be distinctly brought out in the third angel's message; and with that, of course, will come the clearest revelation of the gospel ministry for this time, the blotting out of sin in this generation, thus preparing the way of the Lord. . . .

"And when those truths are preached in the light of advent history and advent prophecy, they will save people from sin and from sinning now. They will prepare a people to stand in the hour of temptation that faces us, and will prepare a people to meet the Lord

The Vindication of God

in the air, and so to be ever with the Lord; and that is the message to be preached in this generation."[21]

One thing is very clear: God is not a dishonest bookkeeper. He will not write "Cleansed" across the record of anyone in the last generation if that person's life has not been cleansed by the indwelling power of the Holy Spirit. Although there have been some through the years who have permitted God's grace to cleanse them from all iniquity, there is a special responsibility resting on that group in earth's last generation who will be translated. Those about whom it

---

[21] "The Gospel Message for Today," *General Conference Bulletin,* April 2, 1903, pp. 53, 54. In an article in the *Review* earlier in that same year Prescott had written: "In this time of the blotting out of sin in the heavenly sanctuary, there must be a special experience of salvation from sin among those who wait for the coming of the Lord."—"Is This the Message Needed?" *Review and Herald,* Feb. 3, 1903, p. 5.

One might ask, Just how does cleansing the heavenly sanctuary and blotting out of sins on a heavenly record have any direct connection with cleansed people on earth? In a sermon preached at the 1974 Annual Council W. D. Frazee handled the question nicely. He said that the work in the Most Holy Place will one day be finished simply "for lack of business." Sinners will go on sinning but will not ask the Lord for forgiveness; their sins will not get into the Most Holy Place. The righteous eventually, by the help of their all-powerful Mediator, no longer are sinning: "there is no more need for an offering for sin."

He asked, "Why must Jesus stand there in the sanctuary with uplifted hands and present the sacrifice of Himself? Because of the constant commission of sin. . . . But the close of probation brings us to this wonderful fact that as surely as the wicked have reached the point of no return, so the righteous have passed the point of no return."—"Then Shall the Sanctuary Be Cleansed," *Review and Herald,* March 6, 1975, p. 4.

is said, "He that is holy, let him be holy still" (Revelation 22:11, KJV), will be truly cleansed people.[22]

All of which brings us back to the main point of this chapter: Is sin inevitable and unavoidable because we are weak human beings? Although we have been studying how the two central truths of the sanctuary doctrine ("an atoning sacrifice and an all-powerful mediator") indissolubly link what Jesus has done *for us* with what He wants to do *in us,* does it really work?[23] Will it ever work? This is the question that hangs suspended before the universe.

This is the question Satan flings into the face of Jesus. The grinding away of the years, decade after decade—needlessly—only adds to the hurt of Calvary and the torn heart of a Saviour who has pledged His word that His grace is sufficient to save His people from their sins (Ephesians 3:20; 5:27; Hebrews 4:16; Jude 24, *et al.*).

A clear understanding of the sanctuary doctrine will change the sad but not hopeless picture. We today have the privilege of entering the heavenly sanctuary "by the blood of Jesus, by the new and living way which he opened for us through the curtain, that is, through his flesh, and since we have a great priest over the house of God, let us draw near with a true heart in full assurance of faith, with our hearts sprinkled clean from an evil

---

[22] "Christ is cleansing the temple in heaven from the sins of the people, and we must work in harmony with Him upon the earth, cleansing the soul temple from its moral defilement."—WHITE, *Review and Herald,* February 11, 1890.

[23] "Our only ground of hope is in the righteousness of Christ imputed to us, and in that wrought by His Spirit working in and through us."—WHITE, *Steps to Christ,* p. 63.

The Vindication of God

conscience and our bodies washed with pure water" (Hebrews 10:19-22).

We truly enter the sanctuary and fellowship with our High Priest when there is a sincere desire to condemn sin in the flesh just as Jesus, our Elder Brother, did in His flesh (Romans 8:3, 4). Claiming the name of Jesus but not His power is not only an embarrassment to God but also the major barrier to salvation. "If those who hide and excuse their faults could see how Satan exults over them, how he taunts Christ and holy angels with their course, they would make haste to confess their sins and to put them away."[24]

The continuing sins of God's people then, as well as the sins of worldlings in general, become a very important element in whether there is anything effective about what is going on in the heavenly sanctuary.

Satan, in one of his towering lies, says that obedience is impossible, that God's laws and expectations are impossible to keep. In fact, one of the flaws of the universe, Satan says, is that God is unfair in condemning those of His creation who disobey Him, because He asks the impossible.[25]

Who is right? God or Satan? When one looks around at man's greed, violence, hatred, and infidelity, it would seem that Satan was right in his charges. It would seem that God either is unrealistic in asking for love and unselfishness or He was unable to cope with the sin problem after it arose.

The issue simply focuses on whether Jesus is able or not; that is, whether He is an all-powerful Mediator. If

---

[24] WHITE, *The Great Controversy*, p. 489.
[25] See WHITE, *The Desire of Ages*, pp. 761-764.

He cannot "cleanse" the sinner from his sins (1 John 1:9), if His "grace to help in time of need" (Hebrews 4:16) is not sufficient to keep His followers from falling into sin, if His heavenly intercession is flawed by an inability to "keep you from falling and to present you without blemish before the presence of his glory with rejoicing" (Jude 24), then Satan is ultimately right. The great controversy would then be settled—God would then have been exposed as unfair, in asking too much from His creation. And He would be seen as incompetent, in not being able to handle rebellion.[26]

Thank God, that is *not* what is happening! Glorious is the news that human beings can cope with temptation and be overcomers. For, standing at the heart of the universe, is the Man who has proved Satan to be a liar. For this reason Jesus had to be "made like his brethren in every respect, so that he might become a merciful and faithful high priest" (Hebrews 2:17); "one who in every respect has been tempted as we are, yet without sinning" (chapter 4:15); one who "learned obedience through what he suffered; and being made perfect he became the source of eternal salvation to all who obey him, being designated by God a high priest" (chapter 5:8, 9).

In proving Satan to be a liar, Jesus vindicated the justice of God. As High Priest, pleading man's case before the universe, He is the living Witness that human

---

[26] As we noted earlier, Jesus had exposed Satan to be a liar regarding whether God's law were fair and whether He loved His creation enough to sacrifice Himself in some way for its redemption. But God allowed time to continue so that there would never be a question again regarding His fairness and His ability to empower weak, sinful humanity who did not have the advantages Jesus had in terms of His divine lineage and special birth.

The Vindication of God

beings living this side of the Fall can resist sin, that God has not asked the impossible.[27] "This was to demonstrate His righteousness . . . , that He might be just and the justifier of the one who has faith in Jesus" (Romans 3:25, 26, NASB).

But the sinless life lived by Jesus was only one phase of the glorious vindication of the government and character of God. The work of grace in the lives of overcoming Christians will be a further evidence of His power and glory. Ellen White emphasized that if ever there was a time when God's people needed "constantly increasing light from heaven, it is the people that, in this time of peril, God has called to be the depositories of His holy law and to vindicate His character before the world."[28]

Ellen White constantly saw this work of the church in the light of the great controversy. One of Satan's earliest charges was that "God's principles of action" were "selfish" and so are all those who "serve God." Then she focused on how Satan's charges are exposed: "To disprove Satan's claim is the work of Christ and of all who bear His name."[29]

In other words, one of the core reasons Jesus came to earth was to illustrate the principle of unselfishness,

---

[27] "Christ imbues men with the attributes of God. He builds up the human character after the similitude of the divine character, a goodly fabric of spiritual strength and beauty. Thus the very righteousness of the law is fulfilled in the believer in Christ. . . . By His life and His death, Christ proved that God's justice did not destroy His mercy, but that sin could be forgiven, and that the law is righteous, and can be perfectly obeyed. Satan's charges were refuted."—WHITE, *The Desire of Ages,* p. 762.

[28] *Testimonies,* vol. 5, p. 746.

[29] *Education,* p. 154.

thus proving Satan wrong; His followers are to "accept this principle" and work with Him in also "demonstrating it in practical life."[30]

Something most significant in the great controversy occurs when the role of the Holy Spirit is understood. So much of Christ's last message to His disciples and the world centered on what humanity can expect from the Holy Spirit (John 14–16).

Awesome is the thought that without the work of the Holy Spirit, "the sacrifice of Christ would have been of no avail." What does this mean? The Holy Spirit "makes effectual what has been wrought out by the world's Redeemer" by glorifying Christ in revealing His grace through His followers. Thus, this linkage between the work of Christ and the work of the Spirit in the lives of God's people involves the "very image of God" being "reproduced in humanity." What is at stake in this marvelous process? "The honor of God, the honor of Christ, is involved in the perfection of the character of His people."[31]

In 1897, Ellen White emphasized again the correlation between Christ's mission and that of His followers in a *Signs of the Times* article: "The honor of Christ must stand complete in the perfection of the character of His chosen people. He desires that they shall represent His character to the world."[32]

The characters of last-day Christians who "keep the

---

[30] *Ibid.*

[31] WHITE, *The Desire of Ages,* p. 671.

"The honor of Christ must stand complete in the perfection of the character of His chosen people."—WHITE, *Signs of the Times,* November 25, 1890.

[32] November 25, 1897.

commandments of God and the faith of Jesus" are the same quality as those of Enoch, Daniel, and *all* the others in times past who became sanctified overcomers, in so doing vindicating the wisdom and power of God.

Job's experience will be reproduced. "According to his faith, so was it unto Job. 'When He hath tried me,' he said, 'I shall come forth as gold.' Job 23:10. So it came to pass. By his patient endurance he vindicated his own character, and thus the character of Him whose representative he was."[33]

Such has been the expectation of God, and the hope of biblical writers, especially when they focus on the end of time when the harvest of the gospel seed is to be gathered in. Why has the harvest been delayed? Such is our concern in the next chapter.

---

[33] WHITE, *Education,* p. 156. See also Ezekiel 36:23–28, RSV.

WHY TIME LINGERS

WE HAVE discovered that the sanctuary doctrine not only clarified the importance of the 1844 date, it also provided a unifying element to many theological truths, such as the Second Advent, the judgment, the importance of the Ten Commandments, the central role of Jesus Christ as man's Substitute and Mediator, the necessity of divine-human cooperation in the salvation process, and the urgency of time in finishing the gospel commission.

Ellen White noted that the emerging sanctuary doctrine "opened to view a complete system of truth, connected and harmonious, showing that God's hand had directed the great advent movement and revealing present duty as it brought to light the position and work of His people."[1]

As the Advent movement saw the decades go by, and eventually entered its second century of existence, the sanctuary doctrine helped to explain why time lingered on, long past the day when Jesus could have returned to

---

[1] *The Great Controversy,* p. 423.

earth. Without this explanation it would be difficult indeed to face the world, as well as the church's own children, year after year, while proclaiming that the return of Jesus is very near. Without the sanctuary doctrine, "very near" would lose all significance after so many years have passed.

After the disappointment of October 22, 1844, early Adventists clarified the nature of the events then taking place, explaining the Disappointment. They recognized that instead of coming to earth to cleanse it in judgment, Jesus had begun the last phase of His high priestly role in the heavenly sanctuary. They continued to believe that the end of all things was at hand. As time went by, their chief concern, as they understood it, was to warn men of the judgment hour and that Jesus was soon to come.

But God had something further to teach His people and, through them, all honest seekers of truth everywhere. What He has tried to teach has been only slowly grasped by His people. This is not because it is difficult, but because it is the doctrine Satan fears and hates most, and the most troublesome for casual Christians to accept.[2]

The reason why Jesus did not come soon after 1844—during the generation that saw the great signs in the sun, moon, and stars—was that His "people were not yet ready to meet their Lord. There was still a work of preparation to be accomplished for them. Light was to be given, directing their minds to the temple of God in heaven; and as they should by faith follow their High Priest in His ministration there, new duties would be revealed. Another message of warning and instruction was to be given to the church."[3]

---

[2] See chapter 4, "The Truth Satan Fears Most."
[3] *The Great Controversy,* pp. 424, 425.

Why Time Lingers

What was this warning and instruction to be given, not primarily to the world, *but to the church?* In answer to this question Ellen White unfolded the deepening significance of the sanctuary doctrine: "Those who are living upon the earth when the intercession of Christ shall cease in the sanctuary above are to stand in the sight of a holy God without a mediator. Their robes must be spotless, their characters must be purified from sin by the blood of sprinkling. *Through the grace of God and their own diligent effort they must be conquerors in the battle with evil.* While the investigative judgment is going forward in heaven, *while* the sins of penitent believers are being removed from the sanctuary, there is to be a special work of purification, of putting away of sin, among God's people upon earth. This work is more clearly presented in the messages of Revelation 14.

"*When* this work shall have been accomplished, the *followers of Christ will be ready* for His appearing."[4]

This doctrine of a prepared people is thoroughly biblical,[5] not something contrived by Seventh-day Adventists.

---

[4] *Ibid.,* p. 425. (Italics supplied.)

[5] In 1898 Ellen White noted: "By giving the gospel to the world it is in our power to hasten our Lord's return. We are not only to look for but to hasten the coming of the day of God. 2 Peter 3:12, margin. Had the church of Christ done her appointed work as the Lord ordained, the whole world would before this [1898] have been warned, and the Lord Jesus would have come to our earth in power and great glory."—WHITE, *The Desire of Ages,* pp. 633, 634.

Many times Ellen White emphasized that our Lord's second coming has been delayed because the church was not prepared for God to use them in completing the gospel commission. In 1887 she wrote: "There is nothing that Satan fears so much as that the people of God shall clear the way by removing every hindrance, so that the

It is the doctrine that Satan seems to hate because it exposes his lies and his defeat. Satan delights in taunting Jesus as He stands in His high-priestly role, endeavoring to represent His followers whose names are being considered in the investigative judgment. With fiendish glee he points out the mistakes of those who claim Christ's name but not His power; with understandable logic of sorts he declares that commandment breakers do not "deserve" eternal life any more than he does, and that Christ would truly be unfair if He overlooks their sins.[6]

Lord can pour out His Spirit upon a languishing church and an impenitent congregation. . . . When the way is prepared for the Spirit of God, the blessing will come."—*Selected Messages,* Book 1, p. 124. See also *Thoughts From the Mount of Blessing,* pp. 108, 109.

Some have referred to this "delayed advent" problem in terms of "the harvest principle." Christ's harvest-principle parable (Mark 4:26-29) is linked with John the Revelator's description of the days just before the Advent when Jesus announces that the time had come: " 'Put in your sickle, and reap, for the hour to reap has come, for the harvest of the earth is fully ripe.' So he who sat upon the cloud swung his sickle on the earth, and the earth was reaped" (Revelation 14:14-16). Compare *Christ's Object Lessons,* pp. 67, 69.

Ellen White, as clearly as words can convey thought, declared that the return of Jesus was already delayed in the 1880s, that He would continue to wait until His glory, His character, is more faithfully reflected in His followers. See *Christ's Object Lessons,* pp. 414-416; *Selected Messages,* Book 1, pp. 68, 69.

Further, in 1901, she admonished church members not to blame God or seek other excuses for the delay: "We may have to remain here in this world because of insubordination many more years . . . but for Christ's sake, His people should not add sin to sin by charging God with the consequences of their own wrong course of action."—*Evangelism,* p. 696.

[6] Satan never has fully accepted the fact that Jesus purchased mankind's redemption through His marvelous earthly sacrifice; that Jesus, through His truly human experience, had proved that mankind can live obediently and without sin; and that committed men and

Therefore, the overcoming, victorious Christian drives Satan to wrath and frustration (Revelation 12:17). Such men and women prove that God has not asked too much of His children when He asks for their obedience; they settle once and for all the great controversy regarding whether God is worthy of His creation's love, respect, and obedience.

For these reasons "Satan invents unnumbered schemes to occupy our minds, that they may not dwell upon the very work with which we ought to be best acquainted. The archdeceiver hates the great truths that bring to view an atoning sacrifice and an all-powerful mediator. He knows that with him everything depends on his diverting minds from Jesus and His truth. . . .

"Through defects in the character, Satan works to gain control of the whole mind, and he knows that if these defects are cherished, he will succeed. Therefore he is constantly seeking to deceive the followers of Christ with his fatal sophistry that it is impossible for them to overcome."[7]

This message of "warning and instruction"[8] that will fully awaken those men and women who look for the glorious return of Jesus has been called, on other occasions, the "counsel of the True Witness," or the Laodicean message.[9]

Such a message is *to professed church members* who

---

women can live in the full assurance of God's acceptance because of the gracious mediation of Jesus Christ (see *The Desire of Ages,* pp. 761–764).

[7] *Ibid.,* pp. 488, 489.

[8] *Ibid.,* p. 425.

[9] WHITE, *Testimonies,* vol. 1, pp. 185–195; vol. 3, pp. 252–260; WHITE, *Early Writings,* p. 270; *The SDA Bible Commentary,* Ellen G. White Comments, on Rev. 3:14–20, pp. 961–967.

erroneously believe that Jesus will save His people in their sins and that there is no need for them to make special preparation in order to hasten the time of His coming.

Ellen White declared that the Laodicean message applied to Seventh-day Adventists as well as other Christians and that its chief purpose was to purify hearts from all sin. This divine application stirred the church in the mid-1850s and most believed that the Laodicean emphasis "would end in the loud cry of the third angel."[10]

But the real intent of that message was not generally understood even by those who were stirred by its importance. Many lost heart because time went on without a great demonstration of the providences of God. They looked outward more than they looked inward for the results promised in the "counsel of the True Witness."

Because they did not truly believe that God expects His people to live overcoming lives "even as I [Jesus] also overcame" (Revelation 3:21, KJV), the "message" could not fully do its work. Ellen White saw the problem: "I saw that this message would not accomplish its work in a few short months. It is designed to arouse the people of God, to discover to them their backslidings, and to lead to zealous repentance, that they may be favored with the presence of Jesus, and be fitted for the loud cry of the third angel. . . . If the counsel of the True Witness had been fully heeded, God would have wrought for His people in greater power. . . .

"If the message had been of as short duration as many of us supposed, *there would have been no time for them to develop character.* Many moved from feeling, not from principle and faith, and this solemn, fearful message stirred them. It wrought upon their feelings,

---

[10] WHITE, *Testimonies,* vol. 1, p. 186.

and excited their fears, but did not accomplish the work which God designed that it should."[11]

The development of character that sets God's people apart for service in these last days takes time. But never longer than one generation. If this character preparation was not accomplished in the generation that went through the Great Disappointment of 1844 (as it surely could have been) then God would wait for their sons and daughters to learn the instruction and profit by the warning that their parents misapplied. If not the sons and daughters, then their grandsons and granddaughters.

But the promise is sure. Some generation of Adventists will grasp this important element in the sanctuary doctrine—it could be our own. They will reveal and vindicate to the universe the mighty arm of the "all-powered mediator" who today stands before our heavenly Father, waiting to make up the people who will be worthy of the "latter rain" and thus "fitted for translation"[12]

Solemn indeed is the description of God's people as they must be in those last days immediately preceding the close of probation. Can words be more moving: "I also saw that many do not realize what they must be in order to live in the sight of the Lord without a high priest in the sanctuary through the time of trouble. Those who receive the seal of the living God and are protected in the time of trouble *must reflect the image of Jesus fully.*

"I saw that many were neglecting the preparation so needful and were looking to the time of 'refreshing' and the 'latter rain' to fit them to stand in the day of the Lord and to live in His sight. Oh, how many I saw in the time of trouble without a shelter! They had neglected

---

[11] *Ibid.,* pp. 186, 187. (Italics supplied.)
[12] *Ibid.,* p. 187.

the needful preparation; therefore they could not receive the refreshing that all must have to fit them to live in the sight of a holy God."[13]

Let each of us ponder his part in this great controversy; let us hasten to accept His forgiveness, full and complete, for sins confessed. Let us not let another hour pass without seeking His power in our behalf for the work of developing our characters into a faithful reflection of His sinless, loving pattern. No words can express how eager Jesus is to save us from our sins, to give us the life of uninterrupted joy and peace now, and to personally welcome us into His kingdom.

Time is urgent for us all. Not one of us knows how many days he may have left, no matter how young or old he or she may be. But even more important than physical death is the closing of probation. It is closing for everyone, imperceptibly but surely. Either a person is becoming more like Jesus or more like the devil. Either a person is becoming habitually more loving, trustworthy, and gracious[14] or he or she is becoming more spontaneously self-indulgent, calculating, and unpredictable. Wheat or tares, the harvest will mature.[15] Every person

---

[13] WHITE, *Early Writings,* p. 71. (Italics supplied.)

[14] "If our hearts are softened and subdued by the grace of Christ, and glowing with a sense of God's goodness and love, there will be a *natural* outflow of love, sympathy, and tenderness to others."—WHITE, *Testimonies,* vol. 5, p. 606. (Italics supplied.)

"The grace of Christ must mold the entire being, and its triumph will not be complete until the heavenly universe shall witness *habitual* tenderness of feeling, Christlike love, and holy deeds in the deportment of the children of God."—WHITE, *Amazing Grace* (Nampa, Idaho: PPPA, 1973), p. 235. (Italics supplied.)

"When self is merged in Christ, love springs forth *spontaneously.* The completeness of Christian character is attained when the impulse to help and bless others springs constantly from within."—WHITE, *Christ's Object Lessons,* p. 384. (Italics supplied.)

is revealing just what seeds (that is, principles of personal relationship with God or man) he or she has wa-

---

"That which at first seems difficult, by constant repetition grows easy, until right thoughts and actions become *habitual*."—WHITE, *The Ministry of Healing* (Nampa, Idaho: PPPA, 1942), p. 491. (Italics supplied.)

"The principles of God's law will dwell in the heart, and control the actions. It will then be as natural for us to seek purity and holiness, to shun the spirit and example of the world, and to seek to benefit all around us, as it is for the angels of glory to execute the mission of love assigned them."—WHITE, in *Review and Herald,* October 23, 1888.

[15] The development of the kingdom of God is likened to a harvest, but not all that matures will be fruit of good seed; in addition to those who accepted the Holy Spirit's invitation, there will be others who accepted the gospel seed but never continued to nurture it; the full-grown characteristics of both groups are compared to the growth of wheat and tares (Matthew 13:18-30, 36-43; Mark 4:26-29). At the time of earth's harvest mankind everywhere on Planet Earth will see the ripening of the gospel seed exhibited in mature Christlike persons living during unprecedented stress—stress caused in large measure by the full-grown product of evil, selfish thoughts and rebel actions exhibited by those persons symbolized by the tares. This worldwide impact of Christlike witnesses declaring God's invitation of mercy and hope completes the gospel commission described in Matthew 24:14.

The whole world will be divided between those who reflect the image of Jesus and those who reflect the image of Satan. For this reason, as the end draws near, evil deeds, moral anarchy, and the breakdown of traditional bastions of authority and integrity will seem to sweep the world into a frightening desperation that will drive men and women to seek their solutions through a crisis-oriented, world dictatorship.

Concerning this worldwide tension Ellen White wrote that God will not allow His cause on earth to be swallowed up by the forces of Satan—the wheat will not be choked out by the tares: "There are limits even to the forbearance of God, and many are exceeding these boundaries. They have overrun the limits of grace, and therefore God must interfere and vindicate His own honor. . . . With unerring accuracy the Infinite One still keeps an account with all nations. While His mercy is tendered, with calls to repentance, this account will

tered and cared for. Soon the whole world will be divided between those who have allowed the seeds of the

---

remain open; but when the figures reach a certain amount which God has fixed, the ministry of His wrath commences. The account is closed. Divine patience ceases."—WHITE, *Testimonies,* vol. 5, p. 208 (1882).

In 1902 she wrote, "The wickedness of the inhabitants of the world has almost filled up the measure of their iniquity. This earth has almost reached the place where God will permit the destroyer to work his will upon it."—*Ibid.,* vol. 7, p. 141.

While the wheat is ripening, that is, while God's people are more clearly reflecting "the image of Jesus fully" (WHITE, *Early Writings,* p. 71), and thus proclaiming the gospel of the kingdom more fully (Matthew 24:14), there is a corresponding ripening of the tares, those who more fully reflect the image of the beast (Revelation 13:14). The time will come when God says it is finished: "He that is unjust, let him be unjust still: . . . and he that is righteous, let him be righteous still" (Revelation 22: 11, KJV). Probation is closed for both the saved and unsaved.

Thus there is that "limit beyond which the judgments of Jehovah can no longer be delayed." That limit is reached only when "the final test has been brought upon the world, and all who have proved themselves loyal to the divine precepts have received 'the seal of the living God.' . . . The restraint which has been upon the wicked is removed, and Satan has entire control of the finally impenitent. God's longsuffering has ended."—WHITE, *The Great Controversy,* pp. 613, 614.

Embedded in God's justice is His concern for fair play. He "will not send upon the world His judgments for disobedience and transgression until He has sent His watchmen to give the warning. He will not close up the period of probation until the message shall be more distinctly proclaimed."—WHITE, *Testimonies,* vol. 6, p. 19.

The ripening of the tares, the closing of the account against the wicked, the ceasing of Divine patience, will not precede the ripening of the wheat, which is the sealing of God's people who have fairly and winsomely revealed the truth about the kingdom of God. The account is closed against the wicked only when they have had sufficient opportunity to hear and to see the truth about God as revealed by those who keep the commandments of God and the faith of Jesus (Revelation 14:12)—and have rejected such a kingdom of obedience and love.

gospel to ripen into the maturity of Christlikeness and those who allowed the seeds of rebellion to flower.

Soon now, this world will see the eastern skies brighten as never before and hear trumpets and a chorus as they have never heard music before. Soon now, graves will open at the voice of the Lifegiver! Soon now, the unprepared will shudder at their coming Lord while earth's overcomers will drop to their knees in pure joy.

But between now and then, all must understand that there is no further probation, no chance to make up for lost time, lost opportunities, after Jesus returns! No future time for character preparation or for some kind of spiritual lobotomy when the Lord will surgically change our characters in the resurrection or on the way to Heaven![16]

You and I are like that young painter in a class that William Hunt, the celebrated artist, was teaching on a lakeshore as the sun went down. Hunt noticed his young artist friend spending his strokes painting an old red barn instead of capturing the glories of the sunset.

Standing by his shoulder, the wise teacher said firmly, quietly: "Son, it won't be light for long. You've got to choose between shingles and sunsets soon. There's time only for one or the other."

For Seventh-day Adventists who have known for so long why Jesus waits, the quiet reminder that we must choose between shingles and sunsets may be the renewal

---

[16] "When Christ shall come, our vile bodies are to be changed, made like His glorious body; but the vile character will not be made holy then. The transformation of character must take place before His coming, our natures must be pure and holy; we must have the mind of Christ, that He may behold with pleasure His image reflected upon our souls"—WHITE, *Our High Calling* (Washington, D.C.: RHPA, 1961), p. 278.

of a commitment that God can soon honor with the latter rain. He appeals to His people everywhere, whatever their present spiritual affiliations: "Join that group who are serious about the commandments of God and the faith of Jesus. Let Me do for you what I have promised. Become part of that people who want nothing more than to see Christ's ministry as High Priest in the Most Holy Place finished. Let Me use you as a living-color demonstration of the winsome loveliness of Jesus Christ. When you do, your life will have just begun."

Could words be more timely?

"Today, if you will hear His voice, Do not harden your hearts" (Hebrews 4:7, NKJV).

Awful will be the words echoing around this planet, one day soon:

> "The harvest is past,
> The summer is ended,
> And we are not saved!" (Jeremiah 8:20, NKJV).

Wonderful will be the chorus:

> "Behold, this is our God;
> We have waited for Him,
>   and He will save us.
> This is the Lord;
> We have waited for Him;
> We will be glad and rejoice
>   in His salvation." (Isaiah 25:9, NKJV).